THE UNFAMILIARS

TIFFANY S. DORAN

PREFACE

He heard their calls every night, but never once did he fear them. He knew then that one of them had gotten a critter.

"Good," Hardy would say. "One less thing I'll have to take care of for getting in the garden. It's finally starting to thrive, so I don't need anything getting in there and messing about." He went on as he slid the curtain over to look outside.

Just then, he saw a large shadow fall behind the big oak standing tall in the back field, its branches seemingly reaching towards the sky as if to hold the moon as it cast its glow across the wide expanse of the farm. It was tall, broad at the shoulder, and lean at the hip. He knew who that was. He was their guardian. Utana, otherwise translated from Cherokee to mean big, was the primary hunter for the group. He would always bring what he killed back to his family to eat, ensuring that the farmland was free of varmits.

It was an agreement that was made between them for them to live peacefully together.

1

Hardy Kilgore, a retired law enforcement officer, had purchased some acreage in the Appalachian Mountains near the southern end. He was ready to be out of the city, the life he had led for years of being a cop, and he was done with having to catch criminals. Now, he just wanted to be surrounded by nothing but wildlife, beautiful sunsets, and tranquility. He began making his life on enough acreage to have a garden for all the vegetables with plans of growing and a nice, comfortable area to call his own. Being a carpenter by trade, he was surrounded by plenty of trees he could use to build a shed, a cabin, and anything else he may need to survive. Once everything was finalized and the property was officially his, he got straight to work. Making a list of top priorities, he gathered all his tools from his pick-up truck and set forth. He used some of the already felled trees to start with.

"No sense in cutting down trees if there are already some lying around going to waste." He said as he grabbed his chainsaw.

He cut several sections to ensure the wood would be healthy enough to build with for structure and support. Finding it to be substantial for building, he started his projects.

The first day was long and hot. The middle of August was never merciful to anyone, so he was glad to see the sun begin to set and started pitching his tent for the evening. Hardy knew this wouldn't be an easy task to do alone and it would take time, but he had all the provisions he needed and nothing but time on his hands.

Hardy was awoken in the middle of the night with a loud thwack against a tree. Then a howl. Then, the call from a barred owl rang out in the pitch dark. Unzipping his tent and shining his flashlight around, he saw nothing but shadowed outlines of tall trees. A starry sky and a -bright moon afforded him some light to see, but he decided it was best to build at least a small fire in the pit he had dug earlier just to be safe. If anything came near camp, maybe the fire would deter it. Climbing back into his tent, he felt a little safer with the small glow of the fire outside. Almost like having a nightlight on when you're a small child.

The rest of the evening was uneventful, and he awoke the next morning feeling refreshed and anxious to continue building. He had made a lot of progress the day before, so some finishing touches were all he really needed. The shed would be complete, which made him feel more comfortable to be able to have a place for his tools. That would also give him more space in the back of his truck for when he had to haul heavier things onto his property.

The next few weeks passed, and he was carving out his own special place that he now called home. He had his shed, water, and his cabin was almost complete as well. It didn't need to be anything spectacular, with it just being him. One room with a fireplace, a small area to cook, and he splurged for an inside toilet instead of just a Johnny house. Sure, it cost more, but when it came to the cold winters in the mountains, he wouldn't be particularly keen on running outside in the middle of the night with below freezing temperatures. It was also creepy out there in the woods at night.

Hardy had heard all the folklore that came out of the Appalachian Mountains. Whistles, disembodied voices, wood knocks, The midnight crawler. He was also told by an older tribal leader that if he gets out in the woods and hears something, turn around, don't run, and don't utter a word about it.

"It could be a wendigo," The tribal leader said. "Even uttering that word puts me at risk, but I have to warn you."

Hardy just tucked everything he heard from people neatly in his pocket, so to speak, and made the move.

Whilst gathering wood one evening before dusk, Hardy suddenly felt he was not alone. The hairs on the back of his tanned neck began to stand on end, and his heart began to race for no apparent reason. He was instantly overcome with fear he hadn't felt since childhood. The woods began to get darker and darker, and he knew it was time to go home. He swiftly carried the wood and himself back to the cabin as fast as his legs could carry him. He was trying so hard not to run, remembering what the old tribal leader had told him. With knowledge of being prey, you're toast out in the wilderness if you run.

As he made it into the door and closed it with a loud slam, Hardy felt that if he were a minute later, something would have grabbed him. He lit his lantern inside and cautiously peeked out the window. He saw nothing. Not even the faintest wind was blowing. It was still in the woods that night. He climbed into his bed, turned off his lantern, and went to sleep. Later, a loud slap on the side of his cabin jarred him from his slumber. Whatever it was hit the cabin with such force that his body shook in the bed.

"What in the hell was that!" he said, shaking as he grabbed the lantern to turn it on.

He listened for a while for any movement outside but heard nothing. He didn't dare to look out that window. He wasn't a coward per se', but being alone in the woods with something strong enough to hit a cabin with that much force was not something he wanted to deal with. Also, what would he do anyway if he saw something outside that could do that?

He laid back down in his bed and left the lantern on but didn't go back to sleep for the rest of the night. He just lay there as still as could be. Nothing happened the rest of the evening, but he didn't get up until the first breaks of sunlight could be seen.

"Surely, whatever did that last night had to have been enormous, so therefore, had to have left some kind of evidence behind." He said as he got dressed.

He grabbed his gun and walked outside.

He was cautious as he walked outside, taking all his methodical movements from when he was an officer into play.

"Always remember your basics. Don't think you're too good to revert to the basics. The basics will save your life." He told himself.

He crept around the side of his cabin, gun on the ready just in case. He chuckled because he knew that little pee-wee of a gun he was carrying wouldn't touch whatever this was that slapped the side of the cabin. But maybe it would be just enough to cause a distraction or even the slightest of injuries to subdue this, whatever it is, so he could get away. His breath was heavy and his heart racing. He peeked around the corner. Aiming his gun in front of him as he made his way all around the cabin, he was relieved that nothing was there waiting on him to snatch him up and do God knows what with him. Once he was sure there wasn't any danger, he holstered his weapon.

"Maybe there is more to what that tribal leader had said," Hardy said out loud, looking around. "Maybe this was one of those, what did he call them, wendigos?"

He had so many questions. "What even is a wendigo, and why can't you say that term?"

The only thing that he was familiar with was Bigfoot. Is that what hit his cabin? It would only make sense as the more he thought about it, the more things clicked.

He had heard the wood knock the first night, the howl, and the barred owl. But were they really the calls of a coyote and an owl, or was there a bigfoot mimicking their sounds? He tried to recall the sounds, and it dawned on him that the owl's hoot and screech were a little off. It was almost the right pitch, but something about it didn't resonate right the more he thought about it. He started thinking about the howl he heard.

That was spot on with the coyotes he had heard elsewhere, but from what he's heard, coyotes always follow Bigfoot. That would then explain the wood knock. Maybe the coyote was following a bigfoot.

The Bigfoot made a tree knock, which then made the coyote howl, and then the Bigfoot mimicked what it's heard in the past with the barred owls.

Carrying those thoughts with him, he secured the rest of his property. He made his way to his garden, which he so sentimentally called his "farm." He remembered living on a farm as a young boy, and it always brought him such great peace. Why not name his garden that here; here in a place that brought him that same peace. It was then that he saw it. His mouth dropped open, and he couldn't believe what he was looking at. A footprint lay next to where he had planted the carrots and the peas. It was human in nature, but the size of it was not human at all. Hardy was the only human on that piece of land, and he never walked through there barefoot. He ran back to his shed and got his measuring tape. Seventeen inches in length and about 8 inches wide.

He was speechless and could only look around and utter the words, "They're here."

Lush green vegetation surrounded his garden. Tall trees of different kinds towered over him. Primarily oak trees, but a few other species were also present. The evening air hung hot around Hardy as he looked around, trying to find an entrance or exit through the vegetation that this beast could come through. But it was almost as if the vegetation opened, allowing it to come in and also allowing it to leave without a trace.

"I reckon I'll have to get one of my trail cameras to put here just in case," Hardy said to himself. "My garden hasn't had a chance to produce anything just yet, but no doubt, it will be back knowing it has free food here."

Hardy ran back to get his camera as well as some plaster to try to make a cast of that print. It wasn't an awful print, but it would not make a good cast. He also didn't have the right plaster, so he hoped that what he had on hand would work. He made a mental note that soon, he would have to build some protection around his garden so the critters, varmits, and now Bigfoot, wouldn't be able to get in. He chuckled at that thought. A bigfoot will go where it wants; no measly little fence will keep it out.

Maybe that was why it had smacked his cabin. The way he had it figured in his mind on the walk back to the farm was that the Bigfoot, if that's what this was, came and was sniffing this place out and got angry that there wasn't anything edible here. Could it have been watching him while he tilled this out and planted seeds? The thought of that shook Hardy. But he had a plan in place, and he wouldn't be deterred from it.

He found the perfect oak tree to put the camera around. Close enough to the garden to get a good shot but far enough away to hopefully not be seen. Hardy put it up as high as he could. He, himself, was only a few inches under six feet tall. Gauging the size of the print, this Bigfoot had to be at least eight and a half to nine feet tall, give or take. So, at the height he put it, it should be fine. The sun had begun to set, which was his cue to leave.

He had already sweat through his white t-shirt, fooling with the print and the camera. He left the plaster to harden overnight, hoping it wouldn't rain and ruin it. He cursed under his breath that he didn't bring anything to cover it with but his guess was that this wouldn't be the last one he would find even if it did get ruined by rain or stepped in by another animal.

Hardy got back to the cabin just as the last rays of the sun were setting. He went inside, got cleaned up, and sat down, happy to be safe. He was still very fearful of what lurks in the shadows. With the print solidifying that he wasn't alone in the woods anymore, kind of terrified him. Again, he's no coward, but he wasn't stupid either. He knew good and well that he wasn't on the top of the food chain out here. So, he must be smart and calculated with his moves, especially at night.

It was a quiet and uneventful evening. Hardy was surprised by that. He thought for sure, with the activity and noise he was making at the farm, that he would get something. So, he put on his glasses, fixed some coffee, and checked the trail cam and the footprint. He hoped there might be more to find when he got there. He walked a little way and heard movement off to his right side, almost as if something was flanking him. His curiosity peaked. The sound stopped when he stopped and picked back up when he began walking again. The woods were thick, and he couldn't see through them to make anything out. He could only hear similar footsteps to his.

He thought he would be slick and took off running to try to trick whatever this was. By doing this, he could also determine whether he was just hearing a medium-sized animal he may have been mistaking to be something large and bipedal.

You can't be too sure in the woods unless you look at it. But as soon as he took off running, the following footsteps stopped and never picked back up the rest of the way to the farm. He stopped in his tracks when he approached the tilled ground. The print was intact and dried well. No rain fell, and no other prints lay inside it to mess it up. But the trail camera...was gone from the oak tree.

"It is getting stranger and stranger here." Hardy said, rubbing his forehead. "I know for sure that was up there tight and secure.

He made his way to the tree and found the camera lying face down. The strap had been broken. He was anxious to get it back to the cabin to see what may have happened. He gently lifted the plastered print, looking it over. It wasn't horrible, but he would have to see if he could clean it up to make out anything definite. He brought everything back to the picnic table he had built and laid it out so he could examine both the camera strap and the print.

He flicked through the pictures on the camera, and everything appeared normal until around three o'clock in the morning. The camera itself began to shake, taking random pictures due to the flying insects it had stirred up with the movement. One shot was facing in one direction, and the other pictures were facing in another. It was almost like the camera itself was being twisted. Then nothing.

He could only assume that's when it fell. He sat it aside and began looking at the print he had cast. He took a soft brush and cleaned off some of the loose dirt revealing toe pads. He pulled his magnifying glass out of his shirt pocket and looked closer, noticing that this print also had dermal ridges. He moved back towards where the heel of the foot would be and along its arch. This was no regular footprint left by a random animal that you would think would live in these woods.

Just then, behind him, a loud crack rang through the forest of trees. Shaking, he laid down the print and turned around. He saw it there. The tall outline of something watching him that wanted him to know was there. It never fully walked out into the open, but it didn't have to. It gruffed disgustedly at him. Throwing everything he knew and had been told out the window, he ran screaming to his cabin. He knelt on his knees and peeked out of the bottom of the window. He could barely see the picnic table from where he was, but he could see enough to tell there was movement.

"Oh, my goodness, what am I going to do?" he thought. "It's seen me, knows I'm here, and obviously, wanted me to know it was here too."

He saw it pick up the footprint cast made and slam it on the table. Pieces of the cast broke apart and flew into the air. He saw his camera fly into the air next and land somewhere in the thick wooded forest.

"Well, I'll never find that again." Hardy muttered, frustrated.

This was absolutely a bigfoot. Hardy took a deep breath. He had always known it, but to see it like this, out in the open, in its own habitat, was just crazy. This bigfoot was smart, agile, undeniable with its build, height, and having thumbs to do what it just did. He watched as it glided around, picking at other things Hardy had lying around. Hardy's trinkets looked so small compared to its hands. It began going through coolers almost as if it were looking for food. Typical scavenger.

He saw it grab what appeared to be one of his small hand shovels and turn to walk away. Finally, Hardy could take a deep breath. He waited a little longer after seeing the creature disappear into the wood line before coming out to investigate. Walking out slowly and cautiously, he made it to the picnic table. He was frustrated that his cast had been demolished. He was even more frustrated this trail cam had been tossed goodness knows where in the woods.

"Well, nothing I can do about it," he said, "I'm certainly not going to go toe to toe with that guy."

He cleaned up the mess that it had made and at least tried to find his camera. He looked for tracks as he walked. Nothing was left at camp that he could use. Grass that had been pressed down in sections wasn't something he could really put forth as evidence. He made his way through the thick vegetation. He looked for hair, tree breaks, and scat. Anything for validation to prove their existence to the world and to prove to himself that he wasn't going crazy. He made it all the way to the farm and came up empty-handed.

No proof and no camera. Honestly, though, if this creature knew enough to break that cast and toss the camera, it would have been smart enough to be extremely careful not to leave any trace of where it had been. He had heard many encounters of only finding one print, not two. Stories of finding prints that lead to nowhere before they just disappeared as if it were vaporized where it stood. The only good explanation he had heard was that they walked backward, making the same step in the tracks that were left.

He checked on his vegetables while he was there to make sure nothing had been disturbed before making his way back. Just then, he heard a small child laughing in the woods. Once again, that fear crept over him, and he wanted to be anywhere else. He swiftly walked back towards camp but stopped dead at what he saw a little way in front of him. More movement, but the figure wasn't large at all. This wasn't the bigfoot that was at his camp earlier. This was a child. But not a normal child. This was a juvenile bigfoot. It couldn't have been any more than three to four feet tall. Fully covered in hair just like the other one, just pint-sized. He quickly started looking around. With bears, if you saw a cub, the momma wasn't too far behind.

2

He did not want to be anywhere around when Momma Bigfoot came back to get their child. He turned slowly around to go the long way back to his cabin, trying not to make any noise to accidentally draw its attention to him. He tiptoed gingerly in the tall grasses. Almost clear of it, he stepped by a tree and CRACK. He had stepped on a long branch, and the sound echoed. He suddenly heard something begin to tear through the woods, knocking over small trees as it ran. It sounded like a freight train, and he didn't know which way to go to try to get away. It was almost as if the sound was all around him, so he decided to stand there until the sound took a directional path.

However, it never did. His only option was to run and run fast. He tore through briar bushes and sticks, not caring about the damage being done or the direction in which he ran. His only concern was getting back to the safety of his cabin. Off in the distance, as he ran, he heard it, a long-muffled yell. He ran faster but then began being pelted with rocks and sticks. He was in an all-out dash, and all he wanted to do was get back home.

In Hardy's haste of getting back home, however, he had gotten turned around. Now, Hardy was lost.

"Shoot," he said, "Good going, Hardy," he muttered. "Quite the pickle you have gotten yourself into now."

He tried to look for something familiar but was so disoriented now that nothing did. One tree looked like the other. All the vegetation looked the same as well. The only thing he knew to do was to turn around and head back the way he came. Not ideal, he knew, but it was the only thing that made sense.

"Is this one of their tactics?" he wondered as he walked. "I think I heard somewhere before that they have this tendency of sending out some kind of frequency, maybe some sort of infrasound. Did they think I was going to hurt the infant bigfoot? They were only protecting it. Almost like a momma bear would protect her cubs if she felt they were threatened."

All this was speculation; he only knew certain things about them, but seeing as how they reacted with such angst, he could only assume that's what the fuss was about. He felt as if he were still walking in circles. He quit looking for his cabin and just started looking for his garden instead. If he found his garden, he knew he would be able to find his cabin since they weren't too far from each other.

He kept searching but to no avail. "Think, Hardy, think."

Just then, in front of him, he spotted a cabin. But not his own.

"How far off trail did I go?" he wondered. "I had no idea anyone else would be here. This cabin must be empty."

Seeing as how the sun was setting, he figured, if nothing else, he could take shelter in that for the evening. He walked around the outside. The structure seemed sound. No holes in the wall or the foundation. It all looked pretty good. He walked up to the front porch. The wood beams were meticulously built. A true craftsman made this.

The front door to the cabin was crafted to withstand any storm, whether it came from rain or snow. Windows sat on either side of the door, so he peeked inside. He was expecting it to be a wreck. Nests of small creatures lying around or something of that nature. But this was a nice home, with furniture and a rug in front of a cozy fireplace. He got off the front porch as he now felt like an intruder.

He walked around the back, looking for the person who may be living here.

"Hello, is anyone there?" Hardy called out.

There, he found a garden and, even further on the property, what appeared to be some kind of storm shelter. He was thinking how he would like to have his garden look as good as this one. He knew it would, of course. It would just take time.

"Can I help you, sir?" a small female voice asked, approaching Hardy.

Hardy turned around to face the lady speaking to him. She was very nice, with a petite frame, and a warm smile.

She wiped the dirt from her hands onto her apron, reached out, and shook his.

"Hello, I'm Emma Jean. Are you lost?" she asked.

"Nice to meet you, ma'am. My name is Hardy, and to answer your question, as embarrassed as I am to say this, yes, I am. I have lived here for a little while, but I was out today looking for something and got turned around. I didn't think I had gotten this turned around, though." Hardy said, rubbing his furrowed brow.

He didn't want to mention the encounter with Bigfoot or his missing trail camera. She would think he was looney toons.

"I don't mean to intrude, but I saw your cabin and thought it was empty. I was going to just camp out here tonight since the sun was going to be setting soon and then head out for home early in the morning." He said.

"Yes, I would agree that being out in these woods at night isn't something I would want to do either. Strange things happen when the sun goes down." Emma Jean said as she looked around.

"If you don't mind me asking, what strange things?"

The winds picked up just then, almost signaling what Hardy already knew to be the answer.

"Strange noises, calls, thumps. That sort of thing," she said. "Never get caught out at night in these Appalachian Mountains."

Just then, raindrops began to fall.

"Great," Hardy thought, "I'm lost, I just had another confirmation to not be out in these woods after dark, and now, it's raining."

"Why don't you come inside? You'll be wet as a drowned rat if you stay out here." Emma Jean said. "I know these storms well. They come in small but go out mighty."

"That's very sweet of you, ma'am. I will take you up on that offer." Hardy said, rushing in behind her as the drops of rain fell heavier.

Her cabin was very quaint. She had pictures of what he could only assume to be of her and her husband on the wall, pictures of children and grandchildren sitting on the mantle of the fireplace, and plants of various kinds sitting on her counter in her kitchen.

"Please, make yourself at home." She said as she went to the kitchen to make tea.

She sat a kettle of water on the stove to boil, picked up her small watering can, and began watering her flowers on the windowsill.

"How long have you been here, if you don't mind me asking?" Hardy asked as he wiped his feet off on the worn rug at the front door.

"About fifteen years or better, I would say," Emma Jean said as she set her watering can down.

She walked to join him in the living room and sat on the couch, motioning for him to do the same.

"My husband wanted to homestead, live off the land. He loved to build things, and he was good at it. It was a good idea at the time, and it lent us all the tools we wanted to instill in our children: Simplicity, gratefulness, skills of trade, family, and God. Our children learned a lot more out here than they would have in some stuffy city, that's for sure." Emma Jean said.

"You have a lovely family. I was looking at your pictures." Hardy said, smiling.

"Yes, they're good kids, we're proud of them. Our son actually helped my husband build all the decking out front." She said.

"I was admiring all of that. It's very well done. I, too, am a carpenter, so I can appreciate good work when I see it." Hardy said.

"Oh, are you?" Emma Jean asked.

"Absolutely," Hardy said, excited to talk "shop." I built everything on my property myself. Cabin, picnic table, if it is made of wood, then I crafted it.

"That is amazing. I know my Archie would've loved to talk with you." She said, smiling.

Hardy glanced at their photo hanging on the wall next to the fireplace. "I can only deduce by that, that he's no longer with us." He said.

"No, you're right about that." She said. "Look, I don't mean to be so open with you, Hardy. I know we just met but I don't get many visitors these days. My children and grandchildren have their own lives. They come to see me, but it tends to get a little lonely out here in between visits. One can only enjoy their own conversations with themselves for so long." She laughed. "My Archie passed away several years ago. Our little basset hound we had at the time, Molly, had gotten spooked by a loud noise one night and ran out the doggy door. I think Archie loved her more than he loved me sometimes," she chuckled. "So, he ran out the door after her. That night was a bad storm: awful thunder, lightning, and heavy rain. He grabbed his flashlight, and out the door, he went after her. Several hours passed by, and Molly came back, but my Archie never did.

"I'm sorry for your loss, ma'am." Hardy said.

He felt bad that their conversation had dredged up that night for her.

"Thank you, I appreciate that," she smiled. "When Molly came back, she had blood on her."

"Blood?" Hardy asked.

"The police came out the next day and searched for him. They didn't give me specifics. All they said was that a bear got him."

"Oh my gosh, I'm so sorry." Hardy said, shaking his head.

"You know, it never did add up to me, though, Hardy."

"What didn't, Emma Jean?" Hardy asked.

"I was told a bear got him but we had lived here for probably ten years at that time, and never once did we see a bear. Not one time." She went on.

"If you don't think it was bear, then what do you think it was?" Hardy asked inquisitively.

"They'd put me in a looney bin if they really knew what I thought. You probably would to. We just met, and here I am, opening up to you like a book and then talking crazy talk." She shook her head.

Hardy knew that she wouldn't feel so bad if she knew what he had just experienced. But he decided to tuck that conversation in his hat for another time.

"Try me." Hardy said.

Emma Jean just looked at Hardy. He could tell she wanted to tell him. It was like an ache in her soul to finally open up about it. He didn't want to force her to talk about it, though. Like she said, they just met. Just then, the kettle on the stove whistled, signaling that the water was ready.

"Would you like some tea, Hardy? It'll help knock off the chill from the rain." She said as she walked into the kitchen.

"Yes, ma'am, that would be nice, thank you."

She brought two steaming cups of tea back into the living room. She handed Hardy his and sat back down. He could tell she was still contemplating telling him her thoughts. She sat down on the couch opposite him and looked out the window in the living room.

"We had heard things, strange things," she started. "Small things at night at first. Trees breaking, weird sounds like someone yelling from the depths of the woods. We thought it was just a big cat, you know. They can sound human-like sometimes. We always dismissed it as being normal sounds you hear out here. Then, we started hearing scratching and tapping on the windows out front. Archie always said it was the small branches from the tree hitting the window, but as you can see from the front, there aren't any trees near the windows, and there hasn't ever been, so I know he was saying that so I wouldn't be afraid." She said as she sipped her tea.

Hardy could see that her hand was starting to shake.

"We don't have to talk about this," he said. "It's okay."

She smiled at him as she lowered her mug back down. "I appreciate that but I think if I finally talk about it, I can feel better and heal better," she said, smiling. "Having someone to talk to about it is nice. Just promise you don't have me committed for it." She laughed.

Hardy laughed. "I promise," he said as he held up his hand, "Scouts honor."

"He would go out every day almost to look around but never really found anything odd or out of place. We never experienced anything when we would go out and tend to the garden, hang up laundry to dry, or gather wood for the fireplace. Except that one time shortly after all this started. He found a small pile of rocks on the end of our deck here. Not big rocks, mind you, just like small river rocks." She said.

"Do you have a river near here?" Hardy asked.

"Yes, maybe a mile directly behind us. It's not big. I'd say it's more creek-like. Not like a river, but there's a water source back there."

Hardy started to put some things together just based on what he knew. Tapping on the windows, strange calls or noises, a pile of rocks that look like they come from a water source. But Bigfoot, if that's what this was, hasn't ever killed anyone that he's heard of...or have they? Maybe he wasn't as versed on this topic as he needed. Especially to live out here. What if this was something more than Bigfoot, like that old tribal leader talked about?

"I heard things I never told Archie about, though. He had enough on his plate, and I didn't want him to worry any more than he already had been. But there were nights that I heard snarling right next to our bedroom window. Like some kind of evil beast was outside, just waiting for someone to come out. We always had the curtain drawn at night, and I didn't dare open it to look out to see what may be making that noise." She went on.

"Snarling, like a dog?" Hardy asked.

"No, much worse than that. It was almost like a snarl you would hear from a wolf, a strong apex predator getting ready to lunge at its prey. I can only assume that if Archie had known, he may not have gone out that night." She said.

"Now, you can't go blaming yourself, Emma Jean." Hardy said.

"Oh, I know. I did for a long time after it happened. The one thing

I can't figure out to this day is, why didn't whatever this was get Molly? Not that I wanted anything like this to happen to her, but she was easy prey. I know my Archie, and I know he put up a fight. But Molly would have been easy pickin's for something like this."

Hardy contemplated, "Well, I would agree, but maybe this, whatever it was, had Molly and Archie come along and it dropped the dog and went after Archie instead."

"Well, I suppose that could've been how it played out, she said. "All I know is poor Molly had blood on her side when she came running back through the doggy door. I cleaned her up, but she had no marks on her. She was just terrified."

Thunder shook the cabin just then, and Emma Jean jumped. The rain that had once lightened up began pouring again.

3

"Have you ever heard anyone talk of anything else around here?" Hardy asked. "Any tales or folklore when you guys moved here?"

"Yes, and it almost stopped us from moving here, but Archie and I decided we weren't going to let what we thought were only tall tales stop us from living the life we wanted and the life we wanted for our children. We heard of the rake, Bigfoot, the wendigo, all of it. I will admit, I was cautious, but nothing ever came of it at all, not until that night that "supposed" bear got Archie." Emma Jean explained.

"Let me ask you this," Hardy said as he sat his mug of tea down, "Do you think it was a bear, or do you think it was something else?"

She thought about the answer before she said anything. Finally, she let out a long sigh.

"I don't think it was a bear, and if we're being honest here, I don't think the police thought it was a bear either. I think that was a "safe" answer to tell a broken-hearted woman. Again, they didn't give me specifics, but some officials came by after everything happened. I could see them walking the property with their weapons out. They never came at night, only during the day. In my opinion, I would think that some of the searches would take place at night, seeing as how that is when it happened. I could only assume they were looking for whatever got Archie. To my knowledge, they never found anything, and the visits eventually stopped. No one even once came up and talked to me afterward, either. I also thought that was strange."

"Wow, well, I mean, I can see them wanting to take care of a nuisance bear, especially one that's lost its fear of humans and become a threat, but that's generally forestry, not police officers or government officials." Hardy said. "I'm like you. I would also think they would at least come talk to you during the investigation, seeing how it was your husband and all."

"Well, and like I said," Emma Jean began, "We hadn't seen a bear around here, not even a trace of one. Whether it be on the ground or in the trees, you would think that by having a water source close by, if we had them, we would've seen them, at least by the water."

"Yes, not finding evidence of a bear makes it strange. You would have at least found its scat, I would think." He said. "How about as of late, have you heard anything odd? I know you said when I got here that being out in the woods after dark isn't advised for anyone. Are you still experiencing things?"

"I primarily garden during the day. I plant, harvest, and water. Any work that needs to be done is all done when the sun comes up. I can't do everything alone like I used to, but what I can do gets done then. As soon as four o'clock hits, I go inside. Most times, it's quiet out...now anyway." She said. "My children help when they're here, my son mainly. He kind of picked up where my Archie left off."

"So, what about your children and grandchildren," Hardy said. "Have they experienced anything strange when they come up to visit and help out?"

Emma Jean snickered. "If they have, they haven't said anything to me, and I can't even tell them what I told you. Sometimes, it's just best to leave it a mystery. They know what the police told us of a bear, but that's all. I'm afraid if they knew what was going on along with everything I've said to you thus far, they would say I was too old to live out here alone, and Archie's passing has taken its toll on me. But they don't even know the half of it."

She got up and moved beside Hardy, catching him off guard. He didn't know what to expect from her.

"Hardy, seeing as how you haven't called me an old koot and run out the door like I was expecting, I must be honest with you." She laid her hand on his knee.

"What is it, Emma Jean?" he asked, turning to face her.

"Well, whatever got Archie is being kept at bay now. It dares not tread anywhere near my cabin. It's been told to stay away, almost threatened." She said sincerely.

"Wait, I'm confused," Hardy said, "It's been told to stay away or threatened to stay away? So, are you saying you know what really got Archie, Emma Jean?"

"Yes, I do. Please, please don't think I'm nuts, trust me, I know how crazy this is going to sound. But it isn't bad by any means. They help protect me since Archie got attacked." She went on. "I feel that I can trust you with everything now. Ask me anything." Emma Jean said.

"Okay then. So, what is all this about," Hardy asked, starting to doubt his own sanity. "What is it exactly that got Archie, and what is telling it to stay away from you.?"

"A werewolf. People call it Dog man today, but to best explain it to you, it's like a werewolf. Part canine, part human, mainly canine, though. That's what was snarling at our bedroom window that night. I just know it. There are several different species of its kind, but this one, this one that was here, was pure evil. With that said, I'm not at all saying that any of its kind are sweet, affectionate creatures, but this was one of the most aggressive ones."

Hardy's head was absolutely spinning at this point. The Rake, Bigfoot, Wendigo, now Dog man? Wow, was he ever getting a cryptid history lesson? But he never dreamed it would be from someone like Emma Jean. He didn't know what to think about what this sweet lady just sat here and said. Generally, he can tell when someone is being dishonest, but she didn't set off any bells or whistles that she was lying about this or anything she's talked to him about since he's been there.

"You think I'm crazy, don't you, Hardy?" she said, waiting for an answer. She sighed and looked away from him in disappointment.

"Well," he began, "I am just trying to wrap my mind around all of what I just heard. I don't think you're crazy. This is just a lot for someone to hear, that's all."

"That's comforting to know." She said as she patted his hand and took a deep breath. "So, let me tell you now why they don't mess with me anymore and why they're not allowed on my property. We have several cryptids in these mountains as I'm sure you've heard and been told based on what we discussed earlier. We also have paranormal activity as well. But what keeps Dog man at bay isn't paranormal, in my opinion. Others' may disagree and that's fine."

Then, she dropped the bombshell of all bombshells on him.

"We have a bigfoot habituation site here, Hardy. They're everywhere on this property and probably yours as well, seeing as how you're obviously not that far away from me."

Hardy took a deep, long breath at that because, at last, he had the validation he needed to know that he wasn't crazy. A habituation site wasn't expected, but at least he knew for sure that he wasn't losing his mind.

"They have a whole family here. Older ones, middle-aged ones, juvenile ones, and toddlers." She said.

So, that is what he saw earlier. No doubt then, it was a toddler bigfoot, and what came crashing through the trees was either mom, dad, or sibling to protect it. It was all making so much more sense now. He was glad that she had opened up about that after all.

"Well, since we're being honest, Emma Jean, this is why I got turned around and lost in the woods when I normally wouldn't have. I had one on my property earlier. I had set up a trail camera in my garden when I found a footprint in the loose soil the other day. I made a cast of the print and set up a trail camera, and the next day, I went back and retrieved all of it. While looking at everything, one snuck up behind me in the woods, but it wanted me to know it was there. I ran and hid in my cabin, and it walked right up, broke the cast, and threw my camera. I was looking for my camera when I ran into a smaller, young one. Obviously, there was a larger one further into the woods, and it heard me and came tearing through the woods, breaking branches, and knocking over small trees in the process. I took off running but got so disoriented. Nothing looked familiar anymore, and that's when I found myself here." Hardy explained, glad to get that off his chest finally.

Emma Jean sat silent, mouth wide open.

"I'm sorry that happened to you. They really aren't scary unless they think you're a threat, and obviously, that one did." She said.

"Well, that's nice to know," Hardy said, drinking the last of his tea that had grown cold. "I really thought I was losing my mind."

Emma Jean laughed, "Oh no, you are not losing your mind. What I need to do is set a way to properly introduce you to them. You're currently seen as an outsider, a possible threat. They're on the defense with everything they do, trying to calculate your next move. So, you say you have a garden?"

"I do, but it's nothing to harvest as of yet. It'll still be a little while on that, but I think one of them sniffed it out and watched me while I tilled the ground to plant my garden when I first moved here."

"That may have been who I call Utana. He is the largest of all of them, and he is also the primary hunter for the group. The one you may have encountered that caused you to get disoriented was probably Luna. She is the caretaker of all the littles, as I call them. She's mostly docile in nature, but she will come at you if she thinks it's necessary."

Hardy sat and listened in disbelief as Emma Jean went through almost a roll call of all of them. "You have Utana, like I said, no doubt he is the one that came to your camp and destroyed your things. If he thinks there's a threat, he will do what he needs to, to protect his family. Luna, as I said, she is the protector of the littles. Most of the littles will be dropped off in a certain area of the woods while mom and dad go hunting. I would have to say that's what was going on when you stumbled upon them. But it's her responsibility to watch over them and protect them. I haven't seen Kaya recently. She is a teenager who is always arranging rocks in certain orders. Then you have the mother who-"

Just then, a loud slap fell on the side of her cabin, making Hardy and Emma Jean jump.

"That's Utana. I just know it," Emma Jean said. "He is the only one who slaps my cabin. He must know you're here." She said as she stood up.

"What do I do?" Hardy asked.

"Just be still," Emma Jean said, "Be very quiet and be very still."

"He won't hurt me because he knows and trusts me, but what I'm instructing you to do is for your safety."

"Would he hurt me?" Hardy asked.

"It's possible, so I need you to listen to me, understand, they are very big and very strong. They will also protect me if need be, so don't do anything crass. Just stay still."

Hardy was as still as could be. He knew that slap well. He had heard it, as well as felt it, that night in his cabin. He hadn't told Emma Jean of that, but there wasn't any need to do that now. He knew who was responsible for it, this creature named Utana.

"Is it a territorial slap?' Hardy whispered.

"It's a recognition slap," Emma Jean said. "He's letting me know that he is aware of your presence, and he feels uneasy about you because you're new. He doesn't trust you."

"Doesn't trust me," Hardy said in a louder whisper. "He's an eight-foot-tall creature, animal, being, whatever you want to call him, covered with hair and can smack a cabin with enough force to shake it, and he doesn't trust me?"

"Relax, Hardy. I understand where you're coming from." Emma Jean said.

"So, how do I go about making him, or any of them for that matter, trust me because believe you me, coming at them to harm them is something I'm not going to do nor could I do," Hardy went on. "What did you do for them to trust you?"

"It took a little while," she began. "It's just like when you first meet someone new. Not everyone clicks like you, and I did, and it takes time for you to build that trust with them. Well, it's much the same way with Bigfoot. At the edge of the porch, where they first left the rocks, I would place my marble collection, just a few mind you, the interesting ones. I would leave them at night, and by the morning, they would be gone, but I would have something in its place, like a smaller pile of rocks or an empty turtle shell, almost like a thank-you gift. It went on like that for a little while. Later, I started leaving bits of oatmeal cookies, peanut butter, etc. Not enough to have them stop hunting their own food, just enough for them to know I had no ill intentions with them." She explained.

They couldn't hear anything moving outside at all now. The rain had made everything wet, making the noises easy to mask in the wet leaves. That sat silent for about ten to fifteen minutes before Emma Jean went to the door and opened it a crack to peek out. The porch light came on, and she could see him behind the tree. She saw him peeking his head around and then he would move it back out of sight.

"It's okay, Utana. He isn't going to hurt you or me. He's a friend, "Oginalii," she said in Cherokee, meaning my friend. He's our new neighbor, and he is very kind. There is no threat here." She said, finishing the conversation. She closed the door and sat back down.

Hardy was almost ready to ask her what Utana had said in reply, and he stopped himself.

"What's he going to say," he thought, "Oh, okay, thank you for letting me know, Emma Jean, and then walk away?" Hardy, you really are losing it.

"You're quiet, Hardyay. Are you okay?" Emma Jean asked.

"My mind is going in so many directions right now, I don't know which way is up. This has gone way deeper than I would have ever imagined. I think I just need to go to bed, assuming it's safe." Hardy said as he stood from the couch.

"Of course, it's safe. You can sleep in the guest room to the left." She said, pointing.

"Ma'am, I appreciate the pleasantries, the tea, allowing me to stay tonight and the wealth of information. I'm going to go lay down and try to work through all of it." He said as he walked to his room.

Emma Jean went to her room as well.

They both woke up bright and early the next morning and had coffee. They went out to sit in the rocking chairs on the front porch, and that's when they saw it. A small bushel of flowers, tied together with a small piece of vine, on the edge of her porch.

"That wasn't there yesterday when I got here, and that was one heck of a storm," Hardy said, "The wind would've blown them away. Did Utana bring you flowers, Emma Jean?"

Hardy was flabbergasted. He had no way of explaining that. It had to have been put there in the middle of the night sometime after the storm passed.

Emma Jean smiled. "This isn't from Utana, she began, "This had to have been left by Luna. Utana leaves the rocks, turtle shells, and sticks. This has a feminine touch, so it must've been Luna. She's the caretaker of "The Littles," remember?" She said, reminding Hardy.

"What does that mean, then?" Hardy asked.

"They got the message I said out of the door last night. They understood that you're my friend and you're safe for them." She said.

"Does that mean they trust me now?" he said.

"No," Emma Jean said, "That means they trust me. They know I'm not going to be dishonest with them, so Luna left these as her way of saying thank you to me for letting them know."

Hardy rubbed his head. "This just keeps getting weirder and weirder. Well, as fun as this has been, I need to head out to see if I can find my way back to the cabin. Thank you again for everything and the coffee. Are you sure I'll be fine as I head through the woods?" he asked.

"I think you will be perfectly fine." She smiled. "Please come back and visit sometime now that you know where I live."

Hardy promised he would and made his way down the trail he came in on. Of course, he didn't realize it was even a trail at the time. He made his way through the briars and thickets. He was so surprised that he had even made it as far as he did. These brambles were bad.

Fear will keep you from realizing a lot. After making his way out of the jumbled mess, he headed back through the woods. Things were now starting to feel more familiar. He still didn't understand how he got so turned around. Maybe it was meant to happen so he could find Emma Jean and learn the truth about the place he now called home. He was glad that even though the circumstances were rough and scary, he had met her and learned all he did from her.

As he continued walking, he started to feel small sticks hit the back of his shirt. He began to become afraid, and the hairs on his neck stood straight up. They were near him. He could sense them.

"I'm not going to hurt you," he said as he continued walking forward. He was too afraid to turn around. "I live here now, too, and I'm a good guy. I will stay on my side, and you can stay on your side."

Suddenly, the fear abated, and he felt okay again. Did that mean they left? Was his saying what he did the reason why he no longer felt small sticks hit the back of his shirt?

He felt silly talking to nothingness, but deep down, he knew it wasn't anything he was speaking to. As strange as it all was and as surreal as it all still is to him, this was his life now, his life with the unfamiliars. This was a whole new lifestyle he would have to get accustomed to. He kept replaying everything Emma Jean told him while he was at her cabin. The dog, her children and grandchildren, Archie, and the awful way he died, and by what? A dog man? That portion of the story was almost too much to wrap his mind around. What even was a dog man, and is it something that he would have to worry about coming to his place in the woods? Then, the relationship she has with the Bigfoot on the property, which he now deemed to be the unfamiliars.

He looked all around, hoping to see even a glimmer of one. They could be hiding in all the thick brush, the trees, anywhere. Since they lived here, they knew these woods like the back of their hand, and they could come out at any time. Was he crazy that he kind of wanted them to?

He finally made it to his farm. He was elated because he now knew he wasn't far from his cabin. He wanted to be back home so he could finish sorting all of this out and make a plan to carry out to start building the trust of these creatures. He was looking at the pile of dirt that would one day be his food source when he saw something almost glimmering, sitting on the tree stump beside it. A marble sitting on top of a feather. The feather was white as snow with only a light grey lining the edges. He remembered Emma Jean talking about how she would lay the most interesting marbles on her porch to find them gone the next morning. The feather, though, was interesting. Could it mean something? It's hard to tell. But he remembers what he had been taught by his grandmother, how feathers, when they fall, carry all that bird's energy. So, it's almost seen as a gift. Could this mean that they knew it was him who was at Emma Jean's cabin last night, and she wasn't just blowing smoke? Assuming they left it, then. Maybe when Luna left her the flowers, Utana made his way here and left the marble and the feather. He picked up the marble and looked at all its diverse colors. Blue swirled with white, and white swirled with pink. It was an interesting one, for sure. But again, more questions than answers. That seemed to be the way with this creature.

4

Home sweet home. He felt so at peace when he saw his little cabin. Hardy was so excited he almost ran to the front door to go in. He sat at his makeshift kitchen table and kept looking out the kitchen window. He was trying to measure by sight just how tall one of these Bigfoots would have been to his cabin. The one he saw the other day was very tall and broad. Hardy could only believe that it would be just about as tall as his cabin, give or take, and maybe about the same width as his window. He gasped at the thought of that.

"Wow, that's huge!" exclaimed Hardy. "There's no doubt that I wouldn't have any weapon to even consider hurting one of them. I don't think anyone would unless it was maybe an explosive. Getting them to trust me is key. I don't want to be on their bad side. That's for sure."

He took the marble and feather out of his pocket and looked them over. He was still bewildered to have found them near his garden. Was it left there because that's where he's been seen before, and they know he goes to water his garden? He wondered what would happen if he put the same feather and the same marble on his front porch.

He figured he would try that. Wouldn't hurt. That evening, he checked the weather before going to bed. He didn't want to put the marble and the feather out if there would be high winds or storms blowing through. Seeing that the weather would be okay for laying them out, he placed them on the edge of the porch.

"I'm just going to lay these right here," Hardy spoke into the darkness. "Thank you for giving them to me in my garden. I appreciate you letting me know that you know who I am. I'm not going to hurt you."

He turned around and went to bed for the evening. The next morning met him with the sounds of birds singing. He sprung out of bed like a child on Christmas morning. He was excited to see if anything came of him leaving the marble and the feather. He rushed out the door. He found his marble and the feather, which had been moved off to the side. Beside them lay the hand shovel that Utana had taken from his camp the first time he had seen him.

"Well, that's interesting," he said as he looked around. "I guess they wanted me to keep these things, but maybe they wanted to show good faith in returning my shovel."

He made his way to his farm. Things had started growing, and he wanted to make sure nothing was hindering them, and no pests were around to dig them up. He decided to scout more of the land he had purchased, this time, not getting turned around and lost. A lot of it was overgrown, but he was still curious. He walked back into the thicket and found lots of weirdly positioned trees. Some were laid out in "X" formations.

He noticed some trees were obviously older and weathered but were in peculiar positions he didn't quite understand. They had clearly been taken out of the ground by the roots, and it almost looked like something had put them back in the ground, but upside down with the root ball at the top.

How in the world can that be, and what sense does that make? Why would something do that? But more so, how could something do that? Had there been some type of machinery back here at one point that could've pulled a tree straight out of the ground and placed it back upside down?

But that hypothesis didn't equate to any type of reasoning either because he didn't know why someone would choose to do that. He decided at that point to just shrug it off until another time, and he walked on ahead. As he went, he tried to see if there would be anywhere a Bigfoot would be able to call home here. There had to be an area large enough if a family was living here. Some type of cave or something. However, he found the creek Emma Jean was talking about, but it wasn't close to her property. This had to be the opposite side of it, he discovered. He was excited about this find and couldn't wait to see if there were fish.

He looked close at the water and knelt to scoop some water up with his hands. It was nice and cold. "Clean, fresh mountain water, nothing like it." Hardy said as he drank the water from his hand.

He walked along its banks. It was deep but not too deep that he couldn't see the bottom. Rocks of various sizes were all around, and he could see some smaller fish swimming. Just then, he heard a strange clacking sound coming from further up the water, almost like someone was hitting two rocks together. He curiously walked slowly ahead, the noise getting louder with each step. Hardy heard movement as well, almost like a splashing sound. With his knowledge of everything sharing this land, he decided to stay back.

He found a tall, wide tree and hid behind it, only peeking his head around to see. He saw them then. A small, ape-like animal splashing in the water. Then, a larger one came into view. Hardy's heart pounded in his chest. He couldn't believe what he saw and didn't dare to move.

"Was that Luna, or was it the mother," Hardy wondered. "Look how massive this animal is. No wonder the noise they made tearing through the woods that day sounded like a freight train."

It didn't really matter which Bigfoot it was at that point; it was just his own curiosity. He was enjoying watching the little one play. It would run into the water on one side and jump and splash all the way to the other. He noticed that if the little one went out of view, the older Bigfoot would click its teeth together, almost as if it were calling it to come back and signaling that it was getting too far away. Hardy was so fascinated by these beings. He couldn't help but wonder how long they'd been here. Did Luna use to be one of the littles that lived here?

How long had Utana been here? No doubt, he then thought, they had to have been here awhile for there to be a whole family of them. He almost felt bad as he watched the innocence they held as they played, basically moving into their home. He decided to leave and let them just enjoy their time together at the water. He started to feel like he was intruding.

As he made his way down the creek, he picked up a few smooth stones to bring back to the garden to place on the stump for Utana.

"Maybe I can start to get them to trust me now." Hardy said to himself.

He found the most perfect ones to bring back and made his way through the woods, past the strange tree formations, and back to his farm. As he lay them on the stump on top of a large leaf he found, he heard a low-pitched hum. The sound of it almost vibrated his insides. He was frozen and unable to move. He decided to use that fear, however, in a positive way, and instead of run, he would turn it into an opportunity.

"I brought you a gift," he said as loud as he could into the trees behind him. "I'm just going to leave this here and go back home. You can come and get it whenever you feel comfortable. Also, thank you for bringing my shovel back." Hardy said, smiling.

He was excited to begin a friendly relationship with them. It was almost like it was just going to be his and Emma Jean's secret. No one else would ever believe them, and that was okay. They knew the truth, and that's all that mattered. Hardy sat on his front deck reading a book and rocking in his favorite wooden rocking chair that he had brought when he moved. The sun started to set, but there was still enough light to see.

A slight breeze blew, and lightning bugs had begun to twinkle around him. This was a perfect evening. He felt such contentment at that moment. He heard a slight rustle in the woods just then. He raised his head and looked around. He didn't feel any kind of fear, so he didn't think it was a bigfoot. Probably just a racoon, rabbit, or something of the sort since it wasn't a big sound. He continued reading. A small giggle off in the distance broke the tranquil silence. He stood up and laid his book in the chair.

"Hello?" he said as he stared at the still, unmoving wood line.

Another giggle came, but this time it was closer. He walked off his front deck and tried hard to see through the trees, but they were too thick, and the sun had set just enough to where the lighting was low. He wasn't afraid. He was getting better at that. Maybe since this was a young one, fear wasn't a factor. But he knew that a larger bigfoot was lurking around somewhere.

"My name is Hardy. I came here to live, and I hope that's okay. I don't want to harm you. I'm a nice man. We can be friends." He said.

Silence.

Hardy sat outside until there was nothing but darkness, and the only light was the moon. He didn't hear any more giggles coming from the woods and no movement.

As he stood up to go inside, he heard a tree knock off in the distance. Then, he heard a higher-pitched yell coming from the area of his farm. He let out a loud whistle in reply. He wanted to let them know he heard all their sounds from now on. He thought it might show his trust in them, hoping they would start to trust him as well. He went inside, got a small bit of peanut butter and a few crackers, and set them on the railing of his deck.

"Maybe, they'll get these before the coons do," he said.

Hardy gave one last look behind him and went inside.

Hardy woke up early that next morning as he always does, had his coffee, and sat out on the front deck reading the paper. The peanut butter and crackers weren't there when he came out, but he didn't get too excited because he knew that almost anything could have taken them. It was going to be another hot day. He finished his paper and looked around at his property. Nothing had been moved or taken that he could tell. No flowers left for him or anything else indicating any of these Bigfoots had been there. He thought about returning to the water after going to the farm.

His garden had started to flourish, and that made him happy to see. He noticed that the smooth stones he had left for Utana were still on the stump untouched. He was discouraged about that. He wanted so badly to have a relationship with them as Emma Jean did. He still thought himself to be crazy for even thinking that. His friends he used to hang out with before he moved would heckle him for that.

"Ahh, look at you now, wanting to be friends with a bigfoot, the so-called keeper of the forest; something that doesn't even exist." They'd say.

But he knew they existed. He had seen them, felt them, and heard them. He walked back to the water, hoping to see them again. As he approached, the low growl came from the distance.

"I wish you no harm," Hardy began. "I just want to come back and enjoy the water."

Again, the low growl crept through the trees. Hardy began to suddenly feel uneasy. That had to be Utana.

"Utana, I left you some stones from the creek on the stump by my garden. You can have them and show them to your family. I'm not going to bother you, I promise."

Heavy footfalls made their way through the woods. The hair on Hardy's arms began to stand on end. He strained to see through the tangled branches of the trees between him and whatever was moving. He could only assume he was being watched. Maybe this was how Utana would grow to trust him. If that's the case, then he didn't mind being stalked. Hardy turned around to go further up the creek. The footsteps followed, and Hardy couldn't shake the unease.

Hardy sat by the creek, recalling that just yesterday, a bigfoot and a toddler Bigfoot sat in this same place. He wished he could get others to believe.

They would be astounded by these Bigfoots. They're an actual generational family. He was lost in his thoughts as he listened to the water trickle by. But a loud knock suddenly pulled him back to reality. He jumped to his feet and turned to face the woods sprawled behind him. The growl came once again. Fear filled his body, and his fight or flight suddenly kicked in. He could see it just then. Movement through the trees. A large black figure scurried through the shadows of the wood line.

"Hello," Hardy called out. "Is someone there?"

The only thing he got in return was silence. He didn't hear the footfalls anymore. He started to think maybe a bear was stalking him. That could have been what was growling at him. But it didn't sound like a bear's growl, though. This large figure was also standing upright. He knew that bears could stand up, but they couldn't glide along as fluidly as this had. He turned in all directions to make sure nothing else was surrounding him.

"Well, I guess I'll head back then," he said to the trees. "I'm obviously not welcome here right now, and that's fine."

As he walked back to his cabin, the unease crept in again. He walked faster. He was hyperaware of his surroundings and heard every bird call. Every twig snap under his feet, and the sound of his own heartbeat in his ears.

"Something just isn't right," he said aloud. "I never felt fear like this, even when they were chasing me through the woods that day."

Just then, everything fell silent.

A large crash came from behind him, tearing through the trees. Something had begun chasing him and had quickly gained momentum. Hardy ran as fast as he could. He turned around only once to see what it may be but could see nothing. How could that be? The sound of something crashing through the woods in his direction instantly stopped. Then, just the sound of Hardy's own running was making noise. He reluctantly stopped. It was a need at that point. He knew it may be a bad idea, but he just couldn't run any further. His breathing had slowed, as did his heart rate, and he stood staring behind him, scratching his head.

"That made no sense whatsoever. I clearly heard something coming after me. That wasn't a simple bluff charge. But there's nothing." Hardy said to himself.

He cautiously started walking back to his cabin again. It was quiet all the way. No sounds and no footsteps but his own. As he passed the old stump, he noticed that the stones he had left for Utana the day before were gone. Maybe that had been Utana chasing him. But that wouldn't make any sense at all. He wouldn't come that hard at him, he didn't think. Nonetheless, he kept walking back to his cabin. The rest of the day was uneventful, and that evening, he sat on the deck in his rocking chair, trying to figure out what that could have been.

Movement came around dusk. Giggling swirled around him. He felt very small taps against the pant legs of his jeans and looked down. There, on the deck, were tiny pebbles. Then, more small laughter could be heard. A smile came to Hardy's face.

"They're playing with me," he said. "These littles are playing with me. The older ones must trust me at least a small amount to allow their children to do this."

He picked up a few of the small pebbles in his hand and tossed them underhand back in the direction they came from. He could hear them running around almost in circles in the trees, and then more small pebbles would land at his feet. This went on until the sun had completely set.

When his porch light came on, he called out, "I'm going to go in and go to bed now. Thank you for playing with me. I enjoyed it."

He heard small footsteps running further and further away from the cabin.

He sat inside at the table and looked out the window while he ate dinner. He couldn't believe that they played a little game with him. He was also surprised that it brought that much joy to his heart. As he was looking out, he noticed the porch light had gone out and then back on. He laid his fork down on his plate and kept watching. It happened once again. He walked out and checked the light bulb, but it was fine. He thought it to be strange but didn't think any more about it. He went in, finished eating, and cleaned up. As he was wiping off the table, it happened again, but he noticed it wasn't an issue with the light bulb at all. A large shadow swallowed the light as it made its way past.

He walked over, ensured his door was locked well and tight, and slowly closed his curtains. He started thinking about the large black figure he had seen earlier in the day at the water. Could this be the same thing? He wasn't sure. He knew though that he was not opening the door back up and was thankful that whatever this was, he didn't grab him when he opened the door to check the light bulb a little bit ago.

Maybe he was overthinking this whole thing. This could have been Utana making sure he was on the up and up since the little ones were just here playing with him. With his size, he was certainly large enough to cast a shadow that large. But for that to happen at all, it had to have been on his deck near the porch light. Hardy gasped at the thought of that. He had just walked out there. He was on the deck with whatever this was. He made a mental note to be more cautious from then on. Even if this was Utana or even Luna, he had to be more vigilant.

The night passed, and nothing happened, for which Hardy was thankful. He walked outside to greet the day, and that's when he saw destruction. He was bewildered. How had he slept through that? He walked over to his picnic table, which had been completely turned upside down. His shed door was hanging sideways off its hinges.

"I must've done something to really make them mad," he said, "I just don't know what. Were they mad because I went to the water or because I was playing with the littles last night? But if they didn't want me near the little ones, they wouldn't have allowed them to come near me first. Also, Utana finally took the stones from the creek. I would think if he were upset with me, he wouldn't have taken them. Maybe this is a bear after all that I'm dealing with."

He continued to survey his property. So far, the most damage was done to the shed door. He guessed whatever this was, wanted in there for whatever reason. Maybe they thought there was food in there.

Hardy turned his picnic table right side up, took the door off the shed, and started repairing it. It took some strength to do that to the door. He was no shoddy an, so everything he made was always built to withstand anything. BOnce everything was repaired and made right again, he headed to Emma Jean's to see if she could give him any insight on what was going on and maybe see if he had been doing something wrong. He grabbed his rifle and some water and headed off.

He didn't experience anything on the way there. No strange feelings, no strange sounds. Just the normal sounds you would expect to hear in the woods.

He met her in her garden. "Hardy," she said, walking over to give him a hug, "How are you? I'm so glad you came by to see me."

He hugged her back and smiled. She could tell just by looking at him that something was wrong, so they went in to talk. She started the water for some tea and sat down with him on the couch.

"So, what's going on?" she began. "Don't tell me nothing because I see it all over you."

"It all started at the creek a couple days ago" he began.

"My creek back here?" Emma Jean asked pointing.

"No, ma'am, it's on the opposite side, so it would be your back half. I can get to it from my side of the property. Anyway, I saw two Bigfoots there. They didn't know I was there, and I stayed quiet and as still as possible. I watched the little one playing in the water, and I'm assuming Luna it. I heard the low hum of a growl then. I figured it was Utana who was telling me to back off. I grabbed some stones for him, and I left them at the stump."

5

"Wow, he growled at you?" Emma Jean asked, surprised.

"I wouldn't say a full growl, almost like a bass singer humming." He went on.

He wiped the sweat from his forehead as the tea kettle whistled. She came back with two hot mugs and sat them down.

"Okay, go ahead." Emma Jean said, sitting back down.

"Well, I went back to the creek yesterday. I didn't see any bigfoot there, and I was just sitting by the creek relaxing. I heard the growl again, but I didn't leave. I figured it was just Utana letting me know he was watching me. For him to trust me, I had to show him I wasn't afraid and that I wasn't going to do anything. But then, the longer I sat there, the more uneasy I felt. Not too long after that, I heard a loud tree knock. I stood, looked behind me, and saw a large black shadow going through the trees. I took that as my cue to leave. But that's not the worst part, Emma Jean."

She sat there intently listening, sipping her tea like listening to the juiciest piece of gossip.

"I was on my way home, and something started chasing me full force, but when I looked behind me, there wasn't anything there, and as soon as it started, it stopped. I passed by my garden and saw that sometime between yesterday morning and when I thought I was running for my life, Utana or one of them had come by and got the stones. Last night, I was sitting on the deck, and little pebbles started hitting my pant leg, and it became a game with the littles. We would toss them back and forth, and they would giggle."

Emma Jean was quiet, almost like she was taking everything inB.

"While I was eating, a large shadow fell, swallowing all the light from my porch light. The light is fine, Emma Jean, which only means whatever this was, was on my deck. This morning, which prompted this visit, my picnic table in front of my house was flipped upside down, and the door to my shed was torn almost all the way off. What am I doing wrong? Are they mad because I was playing with their kids, going to enjoy the creek, leaving the stones? I can't make any sense of it."

"Did you hear them wrecking your place last night?" She asked.

Hardy took a ragged breath. "No, and that's the craziest part. I know I wasn't that tired. I would've heard them ripping that door off. The shed is close to my cabin. It was almost like a spell had been put on me where I couldn't wake up."

"I know Utana has an aggressive side to him," Emma Jean started, "But I don't think he would've done that. Which worries me, Hardy. In my opinion, I don't think it was one of the Bigfoot at all."

"I was afraid you would say that," he said as he drank the rest of his tea. "So, what do you think it is then?"

She took a deep breath and laid her hand on his knee. "I think it was the dogmen that used to run on my property. I know that is certainly not what you wanted to hear, and it's also not something I wanted to have to tell you, but after hearing everything, it's the only thing that makes sense. Our Bigfoot habituation has no Bigfoot that would chase you, growl at you, or destroy your things. Our Bigfoot habituation is filled with peaceable beings. They protect their own, don't get me wrong, but they are not instigators that start terrorizing you for no given reason."

"But what do I do then, Emma Jean? I thought you said the bigfoot keep them at bay?" he pleaded.

"They do, Hardy, on my property. This is a vast forest. They're not going to be able to keep them out of every square inch of this place." Emma Jean explained.

Hardy leaned forward and put his head in his hands. He couldn't believe what he was hearing. How was this even reality right now? All he ever wanted was to be able to move to the woods and live. He didn't ask for a habituation site of Bigfoot and certainly not one that also carried dogmen with it.

"Look," Emma Jean said, "I know this is hard for you to grasp-"

Hardy cut her off harshly before she had a chance to finish her sentence. "I grasp it fine, Emma Jean. I am surrounded by dogmen with a splash of Bigfoot. Neither of which will leave me alone. I'm fine with the Bigfoot. I enjoy playing with them at night, but dogmen, seriously? Utana seems to have only begun to trust me since he took the stones and returned my shovel. But what if that wasn't him? What if that was this dogman as well that took the stones? How long before I truly gain Utana's trust before he can protect me?"

"What I was going to say before you interrupted me," Emma Jean said curtly, "Was that I know it's hard for you to grasp but that I can let them know that one of the dogmen is lurking around the creek. They must know for the safety of their own anyway. For the time being, you can at least be safe there. They will be very diligent at checking out the surrounding woods, so you shouldn't have to worry about your safety getting to it or back. But if I were you, anywhere else outside of that area, I wouldn't ever walk unarmed, and that's for your protection."

"Great," he said, "Just great."

Hardy apologized for his outburst and for interrupting her when she was only trying to help. He thanked her for the tea, and then he headed home before it got dark. As he walked along, he thought of what Emma Jean had said. He felt bad for acting the way he did, but at that point, he had heard enough. He had no problem grasping the fact that there wasBigfoot around. It was the dogmen that he couldn't handle. He knew the behaviors of the bigfoot Bigfoot based on the encounters he had heard in the past, but these dogmen were nothing short of vicious, unpredictable animals. If you would even call them animals.

They were more like hellhounds. He heard noises on either side of him as he made his way through the woods to his cabin. He pulled his rifle, holding it straight in front of him. He turned to make sure nothing was behind him from time to time. That eerie feeling crept over him once again. Was it dogmen, Bigfoot, or just his anxiety getting the best of him? He caught a pungent whiff in the air. Much like that of rotten meat and body odor. He wished he had some way to block the smell.

"I've smelled some bad things in my life." He said out loud, "But nothing like that. Where is that coming from?"

He stopped walking and checked his surroundings, pointing the rifle in every direction around him. He didn't see anything, but he sure did smell something near him. He found that the smell dissipated when he walked forward a little more. It was like a wall of smell located in just that one area. Strange. He decided to just walk on home the rest of the way. He passed the farm and the stump. There still wasn't anything lying on top of it.

He made it back home and found everything to be how it was when he left after it was repaired. He just wanted to go inside, sit in his recliner, and lose himself inside his book. He didn't even feel like playing tonight with the littles. He just felt overwhelmed at everything he had experienced and his talk with Emma Jean. Hardy was discouraged by the whole mess.

The next morning, he woke with a start. He was having the worst dream. This dogman had overtaken the whole area, and he was forced to work for him. The Bigfoot had completely turned their back on him, and he was forced to live there for the rest of his days at the mercy of these dogmen. He stood at the sink and splashed cold water on his face.

"Snap out of it, Hardy," he said to himself. "New day, new you. You've been a guest at your own pity party for long enough."

He made himself a cup of coffee and went out to the deck. He was greeted with the best surprise, bringing the smile he needed to his face. A bundle of ivy and flowers wrapped with twine lay on the edge of the deck. Beside the flowers lay a pile of small pebbles.

"So, it is Luna with the littles at night, and those little boogers left me a gift too." He was so touched by these small sentiments.

He drank his coffee and sat at his picnic table, trying to figure out what to do. He didn't want Luna or any of the toddler bigfoot to fall victim to this dog man if it was coming onto his property. He wouldn't ever be able to forgive himself if something happened to any of them. He had grown quite attached to them. They were a family, too. They needed to be protected as well. Just as much as he and Emma Jean.

He wasn't some brute hunter like Utana, and goodness knows he didn't have the size on his side, but he could do his part. He wondered if Emma Jean had talked to him to let him know these dogmen were treading a little too close for comfort to them. He got up, put his coffee cup inside, and walked to his garden. There, on the stump, he found rocks and a pile of dried grass. A gift from Utana!

Emma Jean must've talked to them. He walked over to get the items to put in his pocket and made his way to Emma Jean to let her know of his gifts and that they must trust him now. As he walked, his hair pricked on end. A low hum echoed through the trees. He knew that sound well. Then, another low growl came from the other side of him. He was surrounded. He had his rifle, but he didn't think it would do him any good. It would at least give him some run time if he shot one of them. He was hoping that one would check on the other if it got shot. That was silly, though. That was humanizing them, and these were not human at all.

The footfalls got closer to Hardy. Way too close for his liking.

"If you don't back off me, I will shoot you." He yelled into the trees.

He assumed just like Bigfoot, that these dogmen understood English, hopefully just a little bit. The footsteps continued, heavier and closer. He could almost see Emma Jean's cabin from where he was standing and decided to throw caution into the wind and make a run for it. Was it smart? No. Did he care at that point? Also no.

He tore off through the tall grass and briar bushes, holding his gun up in the air so it didn't get snagged on anything. His lungs burned. His heart raced. But he had to keep going.

"Just a little farther, Hardy. You're almost there."

His eyes fell on her cabin, and he used one more powerful burst to run the rest of the way. Just as he had crested the beginning of her property, he heard a louder growl than he had ever heard before. It was chasing him, and it was closing in. He was surrounded by woods. Next, a loud roar echoed through the trees. He saw Emma Jean running towards him.

"No!" Hardy yelled, "Go back inside, go back inside."

Just then, he saw him. Utana. He was standing out in the open. He was angry, but aside from that, this Bigfoot was larger than he had imagined. His chest had to have been at least four feet across, and he was pushing every bit of nine feet tall. He looked at Hardy and ran back into the woods. A snarl came from just inside the tree line. Then, what sounded like a whimper from a dog.

Silence. Everything that had just taken place was now still.

He and Emma Jean stood staring at each other.

"Emma Jean, what in the hell just happened?"

"I came running out when I heard all the commotion," Emma Jean said. "It sounded like the world was falling apart."

Hardy wiped the sweat from his face and drank the nice cold beer Emma Jean had gotten him. After that ordeal, no hot cup of tea would help.

"My world was falling apart. My life flashed before my eyes. I had no idea if I was going to survive or not," Hardy told her. "I was walking here to tell you that they trust me now. I came out this morning and found ivy and flowers wrapped in twine, and the littles had left me a small pile of rocks as well. I passed my garden, and Utana had left me rocks and a pile of dried grass. I was so excited, then walking here I heard them. I told the dogmen I would shoot them if they didn't back off. Then it was a full-on war. I knew it wasn't smart that I took off running, but I caught sight of your cabin, and my fear overtook any common sense."

"Utana saw that I came out of my cabin. That's why he came out.

We were both in the sights of this beast. I think he was standing in between them and us. That is the absolute proof you need to know he trusts you. He showed himself to you. He didn't have to do that."

He took a long drink of his beer. This still felt like the twilight zone. Dogmen, Bigfoot, and playing with toddler Bigfoot certainly didn't feel like reality. But it was. This was his reality now.

"So, how do you keep dogmen away?" he asked Emma Jean.

She laughed at that. "Oh, you don't. They do. There's nothing that we, as mere humans, can do to keep these beasts at bay. It must be the Bigfoot group. I had thought long and hard about that myself, Hardy. You know, at the beginning, after they got Archie. Normal animals you set traps for, right? You lure them in, and the door falls on the trap, and they're stuck. This isn't an animal you can trap. You can lure them, sure, but trapping them isn't possible. As humans, only a few things have been passed down from generation to generation on how you could possibly deter them, but nothing concrete and nothing that has been proven."

"Well, I'm glad they trust me now, that's for sure! I would've been literal dog food if they didn't."

They sat there for a little while longer before Hardy set off to beat nightfall. Emma Jean had told him that he should be fine walking home now, all things considered, and that the only thing he should have to worry about now are the typical predators he would expect to see in the woods. She was right. Not a single noise was heard. It was a far different feel to the woods on the walk home. He passed his garden, noticed something lying on the stump and walked over. A black tuft of hair or fur. Nothing else.

"Peculiar." Hardy said, looking around.

He put the tuft of hair in his pocket and walked the rest of the way to his cabin.

Sitting at the kitchen table, he examined it with his magnifying glass. He thought it to be fur more than hair based on texture. It had a fluffier feel to it. This had to have been from that dogman. Utana had left it for him as a gift to say he was safe. Hardy still felt uneasy about everything. But he dismissed it and went out to sit in his rocking chair and wait for the littles to come to play with him. Just like clockwork, he heard their giggles and felt the small pebbles hitting his leg.

"I'm sorry I wasn't out here last night," he said into the darkness, "I was just having a bad day. I don't reckon yall know or understand that but I'm here now, and that's what matters. Thank you for my gift, by the way. It made me smile."

A larger rustling noise came just then, and Hardy frantically started looking around. That whole ordeal that happened earlier still had him shaken. He thought it would probably have him on his toes for quite some time. But he trusted Emma Jean, and he had to trust Utana and the fact that he protected him once, and if need be, he would do it again. Hardy looked out into the darkness, straining to see what could be making that noise, and that's when he saw her. Luna. He was taken aback by the sight of her.

She was smaller in stature than Utana. He could easily say she was about 7 feet tall. She had human characteristics on her face. The more he thought about it, the more he couldn't remember any details from Utana's face. He was too filled with fear to even pay attention. The hair hung from Luna's body. From what he could see, it appeared to be well groomed and clean. But then, just as quick as she showed herself to him, she slinked back into the trees. He went inside after telling them goodnight.

"I wonder if they'll show me the littles, too," he thought as he lay in the bed. "That would be very nice."

He fell asleep and dreamed of the whole thing. Not only with the dogmen but also with the Bigfoot group. He assumed that Luna was the daughter of Utana. He couldn't remember what Emma Jean had told him about their relationship, and she didn't have a chance to finish when Utana slapped her cabin. Maybe that would be their next conversation. Also, who was Kaya? Was she also a child of Utana or another male Bigfoot? He hadn't seen any other bigfoot yet, just Utana, Luna, and the littles, but he knew there had to be more. Maybe now that he had gained their trust, he would start seeing more of them. He hoped so anyway.

His cell phone rang around seven that morning. He hadn't gotten a call since he moved. He pretty much cut all ties. He didn't have anyone holding him there, no family, and he only had a few fair-weather friends. But none he was close to. Hardy picked up his phone and didn't recognize the number. He dismissed it and sent it to voicemail. It was probably a scam call anyway. He got up, showered, and had coffee. He walked to his garden and noticed something was messing with his vegetables. He was angry. They had just started growing. But sure enough, there were empty holes where the carrots had just grown.

6

_____

"Was this you guys that took food from my garden," Hardy yelled into the woods. "I tell you what, let's make a deal. Every month, if you leave my garden alone, I'll lay something special out for you guys on the stump. You are welcome to any varmit you want in these woods, but please leave my food alone. It's all I eat. I can't eat what you guys can. I just ask for deer and my vegetables, please." He went on.

He walked back to his cabin and got more seeds to plant in the empty holes. He covered them up and watered them. While there, he harvested the squash, peas, and cucumbers. With his arms full, he walked back to the cabin to prep them.

His phone was lying on the table in the kitchen, and it rang again.

"Same number," Hardy muttered. "Stupid scammers.

He returned it to voicemail, and checked to see if they had left a message earlier.

Nothing.

"Must not be too important. They haven't left a message." he said.

He went ahead and turned his phone off. No need for it to be on. There's hardly any signal here anyway. It's just one of those things that's nice to have, just in case.

Hardy finished getting all his vegetables taken care of. There was a light tap at his door. He froze. He walked to the door and opened it a crack. He didn't see anyone at all. Maybe he was hearing things. That would make sense because absolutely no one outside of the Bigfoot group, knew where he lived and them knocking on the door would have just been silly.

He poured himself a glass of water, sat on the deck, and read his book. Not too long after going out, the pebbles came. A smile came to his face. He loved when they came to play. He tossed pebbles back and forth for about 15 minutes before he heard them run off into the woods. He went in and went to bed.

The next day, Hardy worked on a small project for his property. When he had gotten everything carved out, the only thing left to do was to sand down the rough edges. He heard someone walking behind him, brushing up against every limb of the trees. Just then, Luna and one of the littles walked out of a proverbial storybook and into his reality. Seeing them together was comforting. Luna was so good with them, and you could tell they loved her as well. It was nice to finally see one of the toddler bigfoot that he was certain he played with every night.

Then, the little one looked up at her, almost like it was asking permission. Luna looked down and gave a nod of agreement. What happened next was something he had never in a million years expected. The little walked up to him and held out their hand. He looked up at Luna in shock. She made no noise but simply turned to walk away.

He took the small, fragile hand of the little, noting how soft the skin was. A small patch of hair covered the back of its hand just as it did the body. Long strands of groomed hair. Deep brown eyes looked back at him as they started to walk in Luna's direction. Hardy couldn't believe that this was happening. He didn't even know if Emma Jean would believe it either.

"I can't wait to tell her about this. She'll be so excited." He said to himself.

They walked further into the woods. They were masters at this terrain. He had tripped several times, and the little that still held tightly to his hand and exuded great patience with him every time he stumbled.

"I wonder where I'm being taken."

Hardy was taking in his surroundings, trying to keep everything he could as close to his memory as possible.

He walked into a vast opening of the forest. There are at least seven bigfoot all around him. In the midst of them stood Utana. There were female Bigfoot and male Bigfoot all in different size. Then of course, the littles. Those sweet little faces all looking at him. He noticed some of the smaller ones were playing with sticks. He saw one pick up an ant on the end of the stick and curiously watch it as it crawled all around before falling off.

"Hello," Hardy said as he held his hand up to wave, "I'm Hardy Kilgore and I live here too. I'm very pleased to meet you and I thank you for trusting me enough to let me come here."

He didn't know if they could understand him, but he hoped they did at least a little. He was also hoping he was putting off the right energy. He knew animals could also sense energy. He didn't know if they were animal, human, or a combination. They had human tendencies and some human characteristics to their faces, but he didn't know for sure what he should call them. Just then, Utana started approaching him. He knew he should feel fear simply based on his size, but he didn't.

He wasn't afraid of Utana at all. Come to think of it, he didn't feel fear around any of them. He could hear murmuring but couldn't make out what was being said or if they were just making noises. He swore it sounded like talking, though, but their mouths weren't moving. Utana came and stood directly in front of him, and Hardy had to look up as far as he could. Utana knelt down, and they were face to face.

Utana face was older. Slight wrinkles at the corners of his eyes, small lines across his forehead, and his skin, dark. He had a nose like a human but flatter and a large brow ridge. It was hair on his body, not fur, and it was well taken care of. He hadn't ever heard of anyone having an encounter like this. Is this even real? He wasn't sure anymore what was real and what wasn't. He only knew he was going to fully take in this experience.

"You're safe."

Hardy didn't see Utana's mouth move. He heard this right in the middle of his brain it seemed. Was this the mind speak he had heard of?

"No matter what, no harm will come to you or her."

He could only assume he was talking about Emma Jean. He was thankful for that. He wanted to respond to Utana.

"Do I speak out loud or through my thoughts," he wondered. "Now it had gotten confusing."

But with that, Utana walked away. They all started walking away. The little that had been holding his hand this whole time, let go and ran after them. Then, they all disappeared. It was as if they dissolved in the trees. Hardy went back to his cabin, grabbed his rifle, and went straight to Emma Jean's.

"It was the craziest thing I had ever experienced," he said as he sat with her on the front deck. "Never in my life would I think that was a possibility. I thought I was dreaming and waiting to wake up any minute."

Emma Jean patted his hand. "Yes, I must say, I haven't ever experienced anything like that before. It must mean they think you are special. They had visited me in my dreams before and shown me things, but never in person. I wonder if they have a plan for you?"

"A plan for me," Hardy asked. "What kind of plan?"

"That I'm not sure of Hardy, but him telling you that no matter what happens, that we're safe, means something. That's probably why he had Luna and one of the littles come get you. He knew that you would freely go with them so he could deliver that message."

Hardy thought about that for a while. Maybe this is what all this had been about since the beginning. Maybe they had to put him in certain circumstances to groom him for whatever awaited.

He felt honored that he seemed to have been chosen even though he didn't know what he was chosen for. The fact that, that had happened at all was still so surreal to him. Being escorted into the woods by a toddler Bigfoot to the other members of the bigfoot family that he hadn't ever seen before was amazing. Now, he somehow had to get to the bottom of things. He made his way back to his garden from Emma Jean's cabin to see if more of his vegetables were ready. Lying on the stump was another feather and what appeared to be an old arrowhead.

He picked it up and looked closely at it. He put it and the feather in his shirt pocket, grabbed the vegetables he had pulled and headed back to his cabin. He sat at the picnic table and closely examined the arrowhead with his magnifying glass. It appeared to be very old.

He wondered if it had been dug out of the dirt in the creek or somewhere else on the property. The feather, he saw, was that of an eagle. Based on stories he heard, he knew that the eagle is strong and brave. The tribal leader also taught him that it was the most sacred and to receive such a gift as an eagle's feather meant that you were well respected. The old tribal leader had many eagle feathers on his headdress. So, what did this mean for him? He could only deduce from the items that they saw him as a warrior from the arrowhead and that he was strong, brave, and well-respected based on the gift of the eagle feather.

He wondered how they had come to that conclusion. Was it because of the way he handled himself in the face of dogmen? The last encounter he had with them, he ran like a sissy, so that couldn't be it. Unless they saw how he handled himself with them in the woods beforehand.

Maybe he carried the warrior spirit around from that, but it would be all speculation at that point. They saw him as someone who could help them with something. They thought he was strong, capable, and brave. Maybe he was deep down, and he just didn't see it. If they went by energy, maybe he put that energy off. Whatever the case may have been, he still needed to somehow find out what they need his help with and what he and Emma Jean would be secured safely from.

He carried the arrowhead and feather inside and laid them on his table with the rest of the items he had collected from them over time. He was proud of that table. That table meant trust and friendship.

That night, he played rocks with the littles again. But before he went inside, he called out into the darkness. "What do you need me to help you with? Are you guys in danger, and if so, what from? I need to know so I can help you. I appreciate the arrowhead, the feather, and what you are saying to me by leaving those. I would like to help you; you just have to let me know how." That night, when he finally fell asleep, he dreamed.

'The sky was dark, and a long band of fog had almost completely overtaken the trees to where you could barely see. Heavy footfalls made their way through the woods, and a cacophony of sounds surrounded him as he walked outside on his property. The moon held its light just enough to where he could see silhouettes hiding behind every tall oak tree. Howls could be heard from far away. Low, snarling growls made their way closer. He didn't dare speak. He felt that if he were to utter a sound, it would mean instant harm. He was frightened but trudged forward. Just then, from his right, one of the silhouettes moved from behind the tree and was now standing face-to-face with Hardy.

It was about seven feet tall, with long fur draped across its body. Its ears were so pointed they looked like they'd be sharp to the touch. Its eyes glowed an amber color, and its teeth were razor sharp fangs. This creature had hands despite it looking like a wolf. Long fingers were tipped with even longer claws, but the feet were that of a canine. Its long torso was sunken and almost appeared to be starving. Others gathered behind this one, but they didn't all look the same. They all let out one long, lonesome howl as they inched closer and closer to him. Just as the leader reached out its hand to grab him, he woke up.'

"Oh no," Hardy exclaimed. "Is that what they need my help with? Is that why I had that dream after I asked them that? Did they make me dream that as an answer I had been asking for?"

He knew deep down in his soul, that had to have been it. There were tons of these dogmen in his dream, but he remembered that there weren't many of the Bigfoot.

"Well, I can do my best for them, but that's all. I am but one human being. I can't take on a whole army of dogmen."

He did as much research on the topic of dog man as he could, and he found some very interesting information. He listened to different encounters from different people. Men, women, and even some teenagers all told of how horrific their encounters were, and after experiencing these beasts himself, he knew everything they said was nothing but the truth. The tall ghastly figures all haunted the nightmares of each of these individuals. Many wouldn't go back into the woods after their encounters, and they were known to be avid hikers, hunters, and outdoorsmen. Some sold their weapons, and others even sold their homes and moved away. Hardy couldn't fathom what he could possibly do to protect the woods from them. He wanted to tell Utana that they had chosen the wrong man. He just isn't what they think he is. But obviously, Utana saw something in him that he didn't see in himself. Back in the day, Hardy was a peacekeeper or tried to be, at least.

"I guess I will have to rehash that part of myself," he said to himself. "But this time, it will have to be with my mind instead of my weapon."

He knew the best way to learn that would be to see Emma Jean and pick her brain about all this. This may even be new to her as well. But she's still more versed in it than he was.

A few days later, he walked to her cabin and explained everything. It still sounded so weird saying it.

"I don't know, Hardy. That's a very bad position to be in." She said worriedly.

"I agree with you, but at the same time, I don't feel like I have a choice in the matter." He replied.

He sat quietly.

"If I must fight against these dogmen...Then fight I will."

Hardy sat at his cabin, trying to figure out what he was going to do. He knew there wasn't no way he could take these animals on with his weapons or anything he had there.

"How does Utana think that I will be able to help them defeat the reign of these dogmen? I have nothing to offer, nothing to fight with, and I'm not an indestructible human being. They'll kill me where I stand." He said to himself.

He went to his picnic table to finish the project he had started working on days before. It was cut, shaped, and now sanded. All that was left to do now was to paint it. Painting had been therapeutic to Hardy since he moved. It cleared his mind and brought him peace. Surrounded by the forest, birds singing, and a cooler breeze beginning to blow. He walked to his shed to get his paints and his brushes. On his way there, however, he saw something that made his blood grow cold. He froze as he saw them.

Eyes peered at him through the trees, watching him and taking in every move he made. Then, it growled and showed its teeth before taking off and running into the woods. It was strange, though. This, whatever this was, made no sound when it ran. It was almost like it had just vaporized and was gone. Hardy had grown so accustomed to weird creatures that even though they scared him, he didn't let them stop him from what he was going to do.

"That wasn't a dogman, I don't think," he said to himself. "There weren't any fangs. It also didn't look like any bigfoot he had seen since being there."

He cautiously entered his shed, got what he needed, and then walked back out. He double-checked the trees where he saw those eyes, and there wasn't anything there. He shook his head and walked to the table to paint. When he was finished, he sat what he had made on his front deck by the door to dry.

"The littles will like this." he said, smiling.

He had crafted a small bigfoot that looked almost like the littles that play with him. He made the hands in such a way that they would hold things. He filled the small wooden hands with pebbles once it was dry.

Hardy poured himself a thermos full of lemonade and walked to his farm to check on the vegetables. He was excited to fix his famous vegetable stir fry that night. He almost had everything he needed. He just needed a few more peppers. He heard movement through the trees but paid it no mind. He knew that Utana would be watching him, so that was probably who it was.

He had thought that it might have been a deer. Hardy started thinking that he would need to go out hunting within the next couple of months to stock up for the winter. It would be here before he knew it.

7

It was growing dusk, and his porch light had clicked on. He walked over to the door and opened it. He wanted the Bigfoot children to know he was there but that he was inside. He thought the smell of the vegetables may bring them in as well. A few small footsteps ran across his deck, and the sound of giggles. He quietly stepped outside, and the bigfoot child who had held his hand that day was standing eye to eye with the Bigfoot that he had made.

He still didn't know if the Bigfoot he had seen was a boy or a girl, but it had laid a purple flower petal in the hands of the Bigfoot on top of the small rocks it held in its wooden hands. In the blink of an eye, the small Bigfoot was gone. He had hoped they would like it and was glad they did.

He closed the door and sat down for dinner. In the middle of the night, scratching noises woke him from his sleep. It was almost like something was dragging its nails down the side of his cabin. At first thought, he automatically went to bear or mountain lion. But he hadn't seen either of those since moving there. There was no way that could be what that was. Was it a dogman that somehow snuck past the bigfoot that was set to keep an eye out for him?

Hardy lay in bed and listened for any other noises but heard none. He crept across his cabin, took his rifle off the wall hook, and returned to bed.

The next morning, everything was still and undisturbed. He made a large cup of coffee and walked to Emma Jean's cabin. He wanted to ask her if she had ever experienced anything like that strange scratching and weird faces peeking through the trees at her. Sitting on the deck in rocking chairs, he slowly sipped his coffee as he told her what had happened the day before.

"It was the strangest thing I'd ever seen. It basically dissolved into the trees once it realized I saw it. After it showed me his teeth and growled at me, of course. Then, the scratching noise. It had to have been claws or really long fingernails, one of the two.

"I can't say I have ever experienced that, but I know someone who has. Sadly, though, he's since passed away. His name was Wally Sandserson. He was a real nice man. He used to have a cabin a little way from me, but he and I became good friends. He had once told me of the same thing; dark figure, growling, then disappearing."

Hardy sighed. "Why does this not surprise me? Did he or you ever figure out what it was? Because that sounds exactly like what I experienced yesterday."

Emma Jean remained quiet. "I do, but it's not something I want to say out loud."

She stood and went inside. She came out a few minutes later with a folded piece of notebook paper and handed it to Hardy.

"Once you open this and read it, do not, and I mean under any circumstance, repeat this word. It's very important." Emma Jean said sternly.

Hardy reluctantly unfolded the piece of paper. He wasn't ready to read a word that came with instructions first. He opened the paper, read the word, and then hung his head.

"How did Wally die, Emma Jean?" Hardy asked.

"That I don't know. All I know is that someone found him outside of his cabin. Whatever had happened seemed to have happened the night before, and he was found by some hunters who came through the next day. That's all I know. With me not being of any kin to him, they weren't going to divulge any information to me." She said as she began rocking again.

She had that faraway look in her eye as she scanned her property. Hardy didn't know what to say, but based on what he had just read, he likely knew what happened to Wally. He was certain Emma Jean knew too. She was just safeguarding herself against it, which he understood why.

"Great," Hardy thought to himself as he walked back home. "Dog-men, Bigfoot, and now this." He said as he pulled the paper out of his pocket. He opened it and read the word again. He thought the word but was careful not to say it. The tribal leader had told him about this before he moved. Skinwalker.

One simple word turned Hardy's world even more upside down than it already was. He just wanted to move out to a piece of property and live out his retirement years. Now, he's chasing monsters. Not exactly the retirement he had envisioned for himself. But he could either accept it or give everything up he had here and move back with his tail between his legs. He wouldn't allow any kind of monster to chase him away. This was his home now, monsters and all.

He sat on the deck that evening and scanned the land sprawled before him. All the work he had done would not be wasted. He stood up before he went in for the night and spoke into the trees.

"I know you know what is going on, Utana. I also know that you may not be able to protect me from this as you do the dogmen. I'll not utter the name, but you know, I just know that you do. Is this another test of yours? If it is, please stop. If you think I'm powerful enough to stand with you and your tribe to fight these hairy beasts, that's fine. But these, I'm of no match for. This is more than flesh and blood."

Hardy didn't know if Utana had even heard him, but he needed to get that off his chest.

After Hardy went in, Utana walked out of the shadows of the trees. He held up his hand and pointed it at Hardy's cabin. A bright light then surrounded it. The light went from his hand and encased the cabin. Satisfied, he disappeared back into the shadows.

The next morning, Hardy woke up feeling energized. He slept

great, the sun shone brighter, and even his coffee tasted better. But he had no idea what had been done for him. Utana knew he was being worn down by everything taking place, and he also knew that the time was drawing near. The portals were beginning to open now, and there wouldn't be much time left. For Hardy to help them, he needed to be fully rested and prepared. He knew exactly what Hardy was talking about, and he knew once the portals opened fully, there would be no stopping them. Hardy walked to the water's edge.

He wanted to see if there were any fish he could catch for breakfast or maybe lunch. He whistled a melodic tune as he made his way there.

The water had a very peaceful and relaxing sound as it rolled over the rocks. He walked further down to a deeper area of water. The water closest to his property was too shallow, but with further investigation, he found an area deep enough to swim in. So, he knew there would or had to be fish there. He cast his line and sat down to wait.

Hardy had spent a few hours enjoying the sun and his surroundings. He had only caught a few fish, but it would be enough for him. He walked back through the woods, anxious to return home to start cooking. He passed the garden and saw on the stump that a gift had been left. A hand-crafted amulet made of a small circle of wood. A small arrow had been carved into the middle of it. But that didn't make any sense at all. Who carved this? This would have taken a tool of some kind to do this.

"Surely Utana's hands would've been too bulky for this." Hardy thought.

He shrugged it off, put the amulet in his pocket, and went back home. After his lunch of fish and fried vegetables had been cleaned up, he sorted through everything on his table that had been given to him. He researched the amulet that had been left and found that it was said to be filled with special powers for protection.

Hardy laughed. He had begun to think this was all so far out there.

"I never would've thought moving out here would put me amid some fantasy land. Maybe I'm just starting to go into denial. I mean, I have heard of that too. Not accepting reality. Denying the encounters. Thinking yourself to be a fool. Yep. But at the same time, I can't truly deny this. This is real, no matter how bizarre."

He thought and thought about everything the tribal leader had said. He decided to do research of his own of these Skinwalkers. As soon as he opened the page though, he didn't feel comfortable going forward based on the small insert he had just read.

The article's author stated that they were putting their neck on the line simply by writing about it. The portion he read was how they become Skinwalkers and then how to kill them...not that killing them was always foolproof. It probably would've been a good, informative read; however, he didn't want to risk it. He was already surrounded by enough. He knew what Emma Jean had written down, but maybe that wasn't what it was.

Maybe it was something else. If this thing takes the shape of primarily animals, what he saw that morning wasn't an animal. It was covered all in black, almost as if it were wrapped inside of its own shadow. It showed him its teeth, no fangs, no fur either, but then it just disappeared into the shadows made from the canopy of the trees. He really didn't know what he had seen to be honest. He only knew that it was sinister and had no good intentions toward him, or anyone else for that matter.

Hardy continued his day and tried to behave as normally as possible. He went to his farm, watered his vegetables, listened to his radio, and read his book. Before he knew it, the day had almost passed by, and the sun had begun to set. He cleaned up his things and was getting ready to go in and slip on his comfortable pajamas when he heard a rustling in the trees behind him near his shed.

"That's odd," he thought, "The littles are always on the opposite side when they come to play. They haven't even been here this evening, come to think of it."

A low growl came from just inside the wood line. Hardy snapped his head around, ready to take off for his cabin. Then he heard it take off through the trees. This time, however, he heard its footsteps as it ran. This wasn't something bipedal, though. This was on four legs.

His first thought went to a mountain lion. That would be the first actual animal he'd heard of this world. That was if that's what that was.

He still wasted no time gathering his things and making his way inside to turn in for the night. He was glad the littles hadn't come to play. They would have been in danger with that animal there.

He decided the next morning that he was going to get to the bottom of everything. He got his thermos of coffee and his weapon, and started walking. He didn't have an exact destination in mind. He was just walking wherever he wanted to go. Generally, his path took him to the farm, the water, or to Emma Jean's. He had so much land he hadn't even seen yet.

As he ventured further into the trees, excitement grew, and he was taken aback by how thick and overgrown everything was.

"How does anything move around back here," he thought. "I bet there are snakes, ticks, and all kinds of things I would prefer to stay away from."

The view was spectacular. He kicked himself for not doing this sooner. Too many distractions. This was living. He went through the overgrown brush and found a clearing in the trees. It was like walking into a different world. The greens of the trees were so vibrant here, and the blue sky was like a mirror of the bluest oceans. Hardy instantly felt uplifted here, and he wished he had built his cabin and things here instead of at the location he did. Off in the distance, he heard the sound of a woodpecker knocking against a tree. He loved birds and walked to see if he could get a closer look. What he found, however, wasn't a woodpecker.

Through an opening of vines, he saw what appeared to be a sasquatch, but it wasn't large. It was about his height or maybe a little taller. It sat down on the ground in front of a stump. Off to its side, it had reached and picked up what looked like a small carving tool.

"They don't have carving tools in the woods. What is that thing?" Hardy asked, confused.

He walked closer to the sasquatch, careful not to scare it. In

Hardy's mind, he heard a voice that was not his own. This voice belonged to a female.

"I know you're back there. You don't have to be afraid; I won't hurt you. I made you the amulet, Hardy." The voice said.

Hardy backed up and considered running. She knew his name! How did she know his name? He had no choice but to think it was from the sasquatch sitting in front of him. He still didn't know how to speak to them.

"The amulet, yes. It is very beautiful, and the carving of the arrow was pristine, thank you." Hardy decided to say out loud.

"You're welcome, Hardy. I know you're also wondering what's happening and how you can help us. If I were you, I would be wondering the same thing."

At this point, the Bigfoot stood up and turned to face him. She was very pretty in the face. Brown eyes, youthful skin, well-kempt hair that was slightly blonder than the rest. He said that she, too, had an amulet. A small wooden circle of wood with the letter "K" carved into the middle of it.

After he saw that, he knew who he was looking at. "Kaya, this must be Kaya." He thought.

She made a sound almost like that of laughter.

"Yes, you are correct. My name is Kaya, and you are Hardy. We weren't sure who would be living on the property near us, she went on, still talking telepathically to him. But once we saw you, as well as the energy you put off, we knew that you could be the one. We had to make sure, though. We saw you go to Emma Jean's and stay there for a long time. Papa smacked her cabin to let her know he had seen you and to ensure she was okay. You had accidentally scared Luna while she was standing guard over the little. That is why she chased you like she did.

It was all beginning to make sense to Hardy now he'd had a chance to talk to Kaya. He wished he would have been able to speak to her earlier.

"Did you guys send the dog men after me, too?" he asked.

She let out a breath of air. "No, we wouldn't do that. They are the problem here, and we need help. My papa can't hold but so many back with his powers. That's why we need your help." Kaya said.

Hardy looked at Kaya in confusion. "Your papa, that's Utana, right?"

She smiled. "Yes, he needs you."

He shook his head. "But there's no way I can help. I have no powers. I certainly can't do anything against the dog men. They'll tear me limb from limb. I want to help, but how?"

"If you look into the sky at night, you'll see it shining bright. A glowing ring from times of past, many dimensions fluttering past. They take a peek and peer inside, of the time of which they want to abide. They all leap in when the portal is chosen, the time of then is now completely frozen."

He just stood staring at her and tried to make sense of her rhyme. So, the dogmen had come from a different dimension to try to take over their land here in the woods, which also happened to be Hardy's property. The dimension they came from then froze in time. His mind was again swirling. This was all too much.

"We need your help, Hardy, because my papa is growing older. He needs the energy you carry. The portal is beginning to open again. Some mean things have already made it into the woods, but my papa can't hold it closed much longer. We can tell that you are brave, strong, and a warrior deep down, and we respect you."

"Mean things," Hardy thought. "That must've been what I had seen in the trees the other day. I wonder if that's all that broke through."

Kaya walked up to Hardy and held out her hand. He lost his breath, and he felt as if he were going to pass out. He held his hand out to touch hers.

"Please help my papa, Hardy. You are our only hope. We had thought that maybe Archie would be able to help, but one of the dogmen got him. Then Wally was taken out by a very evil spirit as well. But, once that portal opens, Hardy, if you don't help him. We will all perish, even you and Emma Jean. The evil will take over this area in the mountains, and no one who visits here will be safe."

Hardy chuckled. "No pressure, right? I would like to talk to Emma Jean, is that alright? She's also my friend, and I need her advice concerning all of this."

Kaya let go of his hand and started walking backward to the stump.

"Go, talk to Emma Jean, but you must hurry. We don't have that much time left. We have been in this area for many years. My papa was a baby when he came. We let people who are of kind spirits live here with us. I know that you have one."

Hardy walked to Emma Jean's with Kaya's voice echoing in his ears. "Please hurry, Hardy, you're our only hope."

8

"Wow, Hardy," Emma Jean said. "I must say that's a lot of pressure to be under and a lot of lives at stake here, including yours and mine."

Hardy shook his head in disbelief.

"Yeah, it's quite the load to bear, that's for sure. Kaya told me they knew about Archie. They thought they would get him to help them before the dog man attack. She also said they had looked at Wally before the evil spirit got him. Now that I think about it, I wonder if these entities knew what they were planning?"

Emma Jean sat quietly. She was no doubt just letting everything Hardy said sink in.

"What do you mean by that, Hardy?" she asked.

Hardy adjusted in his seat. "If the dog men somehow know that the Bigfoot family are trying to recruit help, would it make sense that they would attack them to ensure that they couldn't?"

"Well, I guess it would, Hardy. But what is their end goal in all of this?" Emma Jean asked.

Hardy chuckled. "Look, this is all so new to me, and I can only compare this to what I know. They want to take over the forest. No

Bigfoot to protect the land or the lives of the ones that live here. If they are the only ones here, there's no stopping them in what they want to do...whatever that may be. If there are different dimensions in reality, then goodness only knows what they can pull through. They've clearly already made it to where some other evil things have come through. Kaya said that Utana didn't have the strength to hold the portal closed, and some things have already seeped in."

Emma Jean was just as flabbergasted at everything. He could see it in her face, and he could almost tell what she was thinking without her saying a word.

"We can't let that happen, Hardy. I love it here." She said.

"I understand, Emma Jean. I will do my best as soon as I figure out how. But remember, Kaya said that I have to help them protect everything, including you and me. If I fail..." Hardy's voice trailed off.

Emma Jean reached over and patted his knee. "You'll do it, I believe in you."

Later that evening, Hardy sat on his front porch, letting everything sink in. This was so much more than he had bargained for. He almost regretted moving here. Maybe he should've moved to Florida to retire like everyone else has. But this would turn out to be his fate nonetheless. Emma was also his best friend, and her life was in his hands now. He figured it was high time to quit sulking about this whole thing and get to work learning all he could. Hardy stayed up late that night, learning all he could. He fell asleep holding the book he was reading. He would wake up, read, meditate, and sleep the next several days.

He had to mentally prepare for this battle. This would be a war of the mind more than a physical war. These dog men, not to mention anything else that had seeped through the cracks, knew that he would be of no match to them physically. So, they're expecting to win. Hardy had to learn to overcome fear and focus as much positive energy as he could on taking them down.

Hardy looked up different information on the dog men. He had seen them in the shadows and heard their echoes through the trees, but he hadn't ever seen one. He knew it would life-changing and wanted to prepare as much as possible for this scheduled encounter. What he saw, however, were things you don't even want to see in your nightmares. Seven feet tall, at least. Some were different in coloration or pattern, but the feet were like those of dogs. The teeth as razor-sharp fangs, and the eyes as glowing embers. He had read that some had eyes that were red with matte black fur. He had also researched werewolves as well. Could this be what this really was, and the name had evolved over time to dog man?

The more digging he did, the more he realized that these were two different species. Werewolves were described as wolves but appendages of man. The dog man was actually something that looked like a dog or a wolf but walked like a man. They were both able to go down on all fours, but they were also able to walk on their hind legs. All of this was becoming too fantastical to believe. Hardy felt that if he took in one more piece of information, his head would explode.

He had nothing to do but study anything and everything he could. He needed a break from it all. The next morning, he went to his farm to harvest some vegetables and clear his mind. He almost didn't remember a time when he wasn't challenged with something devious or out of the ordinary. On the way there, he caught sight of something white walking through the woods. He couldn't believe what he was seeing and, at first, thought his eyes were playing tricks on him.

"Maybe my eyes are just tired from reading," Hardy said as he stopped and took his glasses off to rub his eyes. "That has to be what it is."

He kept walking, disregarding what he had just seen, and made his way to the farm. He sat on the gifting stump, taking in the sun's rays and enjoying being surrounded by something normal for a change. He thought of when he was young and would run through the tall corn of his grandparent's farm. The simpler times. Had he known he would face this when he grew up, he would've been sure to hold on to those moments as a child a little longer. He heard movement in front of him, and he looked up. In the distance, he could see that white figure again. It wasn't moving towards him. It was just watching him.

He didn't feel fear, though. All of the studying he had done; he was learning more what some of these things could be. Granted, they were all frightening in their own sense, but now that he knew more about them, he could come at them with more knowledge and not just fear. He stood up and walked closer to the wood line. He wanted to see what this was. It had the shape of a human; however, the way it was standing, it almost looked like its hips and shoulders were disjointed. It had no hair and was white from head to toe.

Its grotesque physique was fascinating all at the same time. How could someone stand there with their joints bent in such a way? It dawned on Hardy then that this must be a Skinwalker. He had read about them as well. He wasn't sure about the shadowy black figure that had shown him its teeth, but he had seen these in the stuff he read.

Hardy didn't carry as much fear with these things anymore, but he still wasn't dumb enough to not heed the warnings they came with. Henry gathered his things and started back to his cabin. He wondered about Utana. Were they facing the same things when they were out here? Footsteps fell behind him just then. Hardy looked behind him, and the white figure was there. Standing perfectly still but watching him.

He had read that the more fear you put off, the more you fed them. You can't emanate any fear whatsoever. Hardy had made it back to his property and walked backward to the picnic table by his cabin. He gathered all the courage he could and got angry. Fight power with power.

"Get out of here. How dare you come to where I live trying to scare me away. You don't hold anything over me." He yelled.

Hardy was proud of himself. Had this happened before, he would've been terrified and stayed in his cabin. With Hardy's words, the skinwalker disappeared where it stood. He shook his head and went inside. Utana was watching from the trees, growing more impressed as the days went by and more sure of his decision that Hardy would help. The thought occurred to Hardy when he went inside that maybe he wasn't going to have to fight all of these entities at one time. Maybe, it would be over the course of time. But what about the dog men? They were all here now. He would have no choice but to take them on at once, right?

Hardy had walked to the water early the next morning to gather the nets he had set out and then returned to his cabin. When he got home, someone was sitting on his deck and his rocking chair. Hardy walked up cautiously, unsure who this was or what they wanted. He had on a park rangers' uniform, but he just didn't give off the vibes of an authority figure. There was definitely something off.

"Can I help you with something, sir?" Hardy asked as he walked up to him after he laid everything on the picnic table.

The park ranger stood up and walked to greet Hardy. "Sorry to barge in here like this, but I tried to call you, and you never answered your phone."

Hardy thought back and remembered the times his phone would ring, and he thought it was some scammers. But how did this guy even get his phone number? Emma Jean was the only person with his phone number here, but she never called. Plus, that had been quite some time ago. Why wait so long to come by if they knew where he lived all along?

"I like this little bigfoot here on your deck," he said. "Did you make this yourself?"

Hardy felt like he was stalling. He felt like there was more to this visit than pleasantries.

"Yeah, I did thank you, so what is all this about?" Hardy asked.

He wondered if this was one of the gentlemen who investigated Arche's death or possibly even Wally's. He could have also been one of the men Emma Jean had seen wandering around her property during the day. If that's the case, then this was not going to be a friendly visit.

"We had reports of some strange activity around this area and wanted to see if you knew anything or had seen anything a little, let's say, "off." He went on.

Hardy knew there wasn't anyone around this area except for him and Emma Jean. There's no way this guy could know anything or should know anything unless he was involved. This added a whole new twist to things. There had to be more than just him as well. According to Emma Jean, there were several. That would mean, based on what she had said, the government was involved in this. This was a visit to gather information.

"Nope, not a thing. It's a great place full of great hiking trails, waters to fish in, and fertile land to grow things." Hardy said with a sideways smile. He wouldn't give this guy a lick of information to take back with him.

"Well," he said in return, "Here's my card. If you happen to see or hear anything, you give me a call, okay?"

Hardy shook his hand. "Yeah, you betcha."

Hardy slipped the card into his wallet and watched him walk away. He was headed toward the property he had just found, where he had his interaction with Kaya. That was strange, however. There weren't any roads or access trails that led to anything in that direction. It was just more thick forests in that direction. Hardy got his fish cleaned and put away, and right before dusk, he followed the same path the supposed ranger had taken earlier in the day. He moved past the stump that Kaya sat at that day, carving pieces of wood. He noticed that it was eerily quiet. There were no insect noises or anything, just the sound of his footfalls as he walked ahead. He didn't know if this were still connected to his land or not, but he hadn't seen any no-trespassing signs, so he kept going.

"There's nothing here," Hardy said out loud. It's like this guy just vanished into nothingness. Maybe he came from nothingness as well. That wouldn't surprise me at all based on the circumstances."

Hardy knew then that all of this was connected. Archie and Wally's demise was swept under the rug. He wasn't too sure what Wally's death was classified as, but he knew for a fact that a bear didn't attack Archie. Even Kaya confirmed that. However, he couldn't go on to say that a juvenile Bigfoot confirmed it. He would be deemed to be delusional. This was either some sort of cover-up by the actual government or, there was a government all its own over these creatures. Possibly from the same dimension they came from. Either way, Hardy was determined to get to the bottom of it. Especially if he was the one who held the key to all of it.

He showed Emma Jean the card the next day. He had toyed with the idea of showing her all night after he had gotten back home. He didn't want to dredge everything up that she had already gone through with Archie, but he knew that she too, was probably given a card with the same instructions to call.

"It looked like a legitimate business card," Emma Jean said. "I never had a reason to question it. They were all dressed as park rangers. I did find their actions peculiar, but I was just recently widowed, a heartbroken mess. Who was I at that time to question them?"

Hardy sighed. "That I get, but now, it's different. We both know that a bear didn't attack him, and we know that Wally was killed by this evil spirit. Now, since everything has started with me learning more and more about these entities and having them on the property, I get a visit. I don't see that as a coincidence, Emma Jean, I just don't."

She got up, fixed some tea, and sat back down at the table across from Hardy. "Look, that I agree with, but you realize that now, they're stalking you, so to speak."

Hardy laughed. "I have everything stalking me at this point. It doesn't matter. I have bigfoot, dog men, whatever that white thing was the other day, now, creepy supposed forest rangers. Nothing surprises me anymore."

"Yes, tell me more about that white figure you saw. Didn't you see that yesterday, which happened to be the same day the ranger came?"

Hardy hadn't thought about that, but she was right. Directly after almost.

"It was actually the next day; I had just come back from gathering my fish, and he was there when I got home. He was sitting on my deck waiting for me. I wonder how long he had been there, honestly. I had spent a lot of time at the water. I had seen the white figure the day before when I went to get some of my vegetables. It was off to my right in the trees on my way down there. In an instant, it was in front of me in the trees, and then when I had nearly reached my cabin, it was directly behind me." Hardy said.

"Was it a ghost, ya think?" she asked.

"No, this wasn't a ghost at all. Whatever this was, it was a solid being. I felt like I could just reach out and touch it if I wanted to. There wasn't any transparency at all. It dissolved almost immediately afterwards when I was forceful with it and showed no fear. That part was odd."

She leaned back in her chair and sipped her tea. "I think Utana is losing more and more of his grip on this version of reality, and more things are getting through. That has to be the explanation. Whoever these fake rangers are probably know that. Truth be told, this could have been going on long before you or I even came here. I didn't know anything like this even existed. I only knew what I was told. Now look at me. Right in the heart of it with you."

Hardy knew she was probably right. "Do you think these rangers are along the lines of the men in black? I read about them when I was doing some research. The men in black, however, generally show up in business suits. What if the rangers are of the same bunch but have to dress accordingly since we're in the woods?"

"I guess that could always be an explanation as well. They come to see what people know or what they've seen. You know he had to have known you were lying." Emma Jean said.

"I just don't understand why they hadn't showed up until now. Granted, he said they had tried to call me after I had already experienced some things. But I also don't understand that aspect of it either. How did they even get my number?" Hardy asked.

"Well, let's think this through. If they are some form of government, they already have your information. I think it's a group of them. They could even disguise themselves as actual government officials to access your information that way, too. That would explain how they got your phone number and knew where your cabin is as well. We can go off-grid as much as we want, but they all still know where we are." Emma Jean said.

Hardy knew she was right. From now on, he would have to be more vigilant of all the pops and cracks he heard in the woods. Maybe they were spying on him. Maybe not all the noises he heard were of bigfoot or anything else strange. They could be footsteps made by these fake officials. In his opinion, they had to have some sort of cryptid in them. Maybe even something extraterrestrial. That was a rabbit hole he didn't want to travel down. He didn't think he could handle alien invasions on top of everything else. What he was having to deal with was enough.

Hardy left Emma Jean's and walked past his garden. He saw a small pile of pebbles lying on the stump with a purple flower pedal on top. He knew this was a gift from the littles, but why had they left it here and not in the hands of the wooden bigfoot on his deck as before? He picked them up and put them all in his pocket for safe-keeping. When he got home, he saw why they left it there instead. The small wooden bigfoot he had crafted with his hands had been broken in half. An intentional attack on his property, but from what... or who? No wonder the littles had left that at the stump. They knew it wasn't safe, and maybe, it was a warning for him to let him know what had happened and be on guard.

The more Hardy thought about it, nothing had happened to that little bigfoot until the ranger came by yesterday, and he physically touched it. Maybe that had something to do with the attack.

Hardy took the bigfoot off his deck and put it inside his shed. A gust of wind blew hard around him when he closed his shed. It was almost like a whirlwind tornado blowing everything around. But as soon as it started, it once again stopped. Hardy decided at that time that it was best that he go in. He knew a lot more about things than he did before, but not enough to chance it at the same time. He hadn't ever experienced or read about this gust of wind.

That night, a loud whistle came from the woods.

That was a bigfoot whistle, and he knew it well. It was Utana. Hardy cautiously walked outside armed with his flashlight and his weapon just to be on the safe side. He stood on the deck and waited for anything to come to him. A voice in his head, seeing Utana standing in front of him, something. That whistle was a warning whistle. Something dangerous was out here. Hardy just didn't know what. He stood with his back to the door so nothing could come in from behind him, and he had the quickest way in as possible if he was charged from the front. Just then, he heard Utana's voice.

"The time is drawing nearer than ever. The portal opened today, letting more inside our world. The ranger who came to see you also comes from that world. Danger is here in our land. The seam to the veil has been torn, and you are now in a position to help us." Utana said.

"Help you, help you how," Hardy asked. "Yes, I've been studying and feel more confident, but how in the world can I close a supernatural portal?"

Utana grunted. "It's not about the portal, Hardy. It's about you. It's always been about you. They know it. You have survived more than you were supposed to. You have the key to their undoing."

Another strong wind came just then, swirling around Hardy as it did earlier that day. However, this time, something evil stood before him just at the bottom of his steps. Fear overtook Hardy, and without even thinking, he fired his gun. The shot echoed through the forest, and this evil being that had once stood now lay on the ground, not moving. Hardy wished he had more light to see this thing with.

But all he had was the dim glow from his porchlight and the flashlight he held. He moved forward hesitantly away from the door and tried to get a closer look at the body. It was disjointed, just like the white figure he saw before, but this one didn't look like a person. This was more like an animal. He still hadn't seen any movement, so he moved closer and closer down the stairs towards it.

"You can kill these things with bullets," Hardy asked out loud. "Well, that's very anticlimactic. I would have thought I needed to do some ritual to take care of these."

Hardy was right in the sense that bullets could kill them but it had to be a certain type of bullet. Ash bullets. Unbeknownst to Hardy, Luna had switched his out for these the last time he loaded his weapon. But now the problem came that he had a body on his property that he had just killed. Utana had been quiet since the gunshot rang out. Hardy felt safe enough to go inside to see what he had that he could at least cover it with until morning. When he came back out, though, the body of whatever this disjointed thing was, was gone. Nowhere to be seen. Hardy reluctantly searched everywhere, minus the woods. Of course, he wasn't that brave yet. This thing had vanished, like it had never been there.

"Well, that's not surprising," Hardy said. "Anymore, this kind of thing is normal."

The next morning, a knock on his door woke him. He was confused as to who would be there. He never had any visitors. Well, of the normal kind, that is. He fumbled to put his glasses on and walked to the door.

It was the park ranger again. Hardy sighed at the sight of him. "Can I help you, sir?"

"Good morning, pal," the ranger said exuberantly. "We had a report of gunfire from your house last night, and we wanted to make sure you were okay."

Hardy looked past him and saw that he was alone. "With all due respect, what's this we stuff, sir? There's no one here but you."

The ranger chuckled. "Ahh, yes, we are all back at the ranger station."

Hardy took a closer look at him. His face was pale, very thin. He almost looked sickly. His ears were pinned back very close to his head. He held the words that Utana had told him the night before in the forefront of his mind. "The ranger who came to see you is also from that world."

Knowing this, Hardy knew he still had to play the innocence card. He knew just what to say, too, to hopefully ruffle his feathers.

"Yeah, I heard something rummaging around my cabin here, and when I came out, I saw a bear nosing in my trash can. One shot and it took off, problem solved." Hardy winked.

The ranger eyed him. He knew the truth, and Hardy could read him like a book. The ranger's face went from a happy smile to holding an angry expression. Hardy was wearing him down, and it was starting to show. Like taking candy from a baby. They had to know he knew more than he was saying, but at the same time, they couldn't risk it just in case he didn't.

"Well, sir, you just keep your eyes open, especially if you've seen a bear. There's always more than one." he said with a return wink to Hardy.

Hardy knew exactly what that meant. He just had to keep playing the game. Hardy walked to the water to read that day. Change of scenery, and it would be relaxing to listen to the waterfall over the rocks while he was reading. He had made it almost the rest of the way through his story when he heard several knocks coming from Emma Jeans' direction. He thought they might just be letting her know they were there and she was safe. He really hoped that the rangers wouldn't start giving her a hard time, too. She didn't deserve that, and they should know from previous interactions with her that she isn't going to help them either. A loud whistle came next. One that brought Hardy to full attention. The growling started next. That was a protection knock, after all, then the whistle to follow. They're warning both of us that a dog man is in the area. That's exactly what that was. Hardy ran by the creek to Emma Jean's house.

When Hardy got to Emma Jean's house, his heart sank. On her front deck were streaks of blood.

Hardy banged on her door and screamed her name.

"Emma Jean, where are you? Are you okay?"

He went around her property and found nothing. He got into her back door and searched her whole house, but she was nowhere to be seen. He did notice, however, that there wasn't any blood inside. That was a relief, at least, but it still didn't answer the question of where she was. He feared the worst, as anyone would at that point.

"What if they attacked her on the front porch and dragged her into the woods," Hardy thought as his heart raced. "I have to find her, no matter the cost."

Hardy took off running into the thick vegetation of the woods that surrounded Emma Jeans. He was frantic at this point, damn near pulling everything down with his bare hands to get through. He continuously called her name, but no reply ever came back. Silence surrounded him as he stood in the middle of a clearing in the woods to catch his breath. He was near tears at this point, and his adrenaline was higher than ever.

"Where were Utana and the other bigfoot in the group supposed to protect us?" Hardy thought.

A loud whistle rang out again through the trees coming from the direction of Emma Jeans. Hardy ran as fast as he could back, still not caring for his own safety. Utana stepped out from behind a tree in the back near the cabin. It was then that Hardy saw it. The storm cellar, of course! Hardy ran over to it and tried to open the doors, but they were locked. He pounded hard on the door with his fists.

"Emma Jean, it's Hardy, please. Are you in there? If you are, please open the doors."

I was t for a while, and then he heard the locks rattle from inside the house. He was relieved. He crawled down in there with Emma Jean as she pushed the doors open a little bit and hugged her as tight as he could.

"Are you okay? I saw the blood on your front porch, and then I couldn't find you. I ran through the woods and everything looking. Utana led me to you."

"I'm fine, but they came to the door. I thought it was a ranger, but it wasn't truly a ranger, Hardy. It was a shapeshifter. It changed right in front of my eyes. I took off running and tripped on my rug. When I fell, it grabbed my leg and was trying to pull me towards it. With it pulling me and me trying to pull away, its nails dug into my skin. I ran through the house and went to my storm shelter, the safest place I knew. I locked myself inside, waiting for whatever this was to go away or for Utana to come out."

Hardy sighed and shook his head. "This is getting worse and

worse. I'm damn tired of it too. I am the key to all of it. Only I can kill them. That's what I intend to do from now on. Anything I see is going to eat a bullet."

Three knocks from a tree came then. Emma Jean and Hardy peered out of the crack of the storm cellar door. They saw Utana standing just behind the big oak tree by Emma Jean's cabin. Feeling it was safe, they both crawled out and made their way inside.

9

Hardy went into the kitchen after he and Emma Jean came in. He started the tea so she could sit down and prop her foot up, and he grabbed a beer. He was mentally exhausted after that whole ordeal. He thought for sure that these monsters had gotten his friend. He was elated that she was still here and mustered enough strength to pull out their grasps.

"As you know after finding out the hard way, these park rangers are not what they say they are," Hardy said. "As you said yourself, they're shapeshifters. I wonder if they all are or if it's only a few. Utana came to me and told me that the veil had been torn and the portal had opened. The ranger that came to see me is also a part of the world everything is coming from. The white figure I had seen days prior came to my house last night. I shot it with my rifle and killed it. By the time I went in to get something to cover it and come back out, it was gone. Then, this morning, the ranger showed up asking about the gunshot that was fired."

Emma Jean gasped. "Hardy, that's frightening. What did you tell him?"

"I gave him a dose of his own medicine and told him it was a bear in my trash," Hardy laughed. "He was so mad because I'm just not coming off of the information he wants to know."

The tea kettle whistled, and Hardy got up to fix her cup of tea and get some bandages and medicine to clean up her leg.

"Yeah, he was spitting mad, Hardy continued as he sat back down. "I'm breaking him down slowly but surely. I want to see what he will do when and if he snaps."

"Well, take it from me, Hardy," Emma Jean said, pointing to her leg he had just bandaged, "They're not nice at all, and they will seemingly stop at nothing to get you. I'm just glad I was able to get away. There's no doubt in my mind that if I hadn't, I wouldn't be sitting here with you now."

Hardy shuddered at that thought. He would be lost without Emma Jean. She was his best friend and the only friend he had out here, except for the bigfoot, but the only human friend he had out here. They would absolutely have to be extremely careful. He feared that Emma Jean would have to be more careful than he would because now, she's seen them for who they truly were. Seeing as how he and Emma Jean were such close friends, they had to know that they would talk, and she would tell him. This would not be fun at all, and he needed some kind of guidance to push forward with this. They wouldn't take to his smart-alec tone for much longer. If they were brazening enough to change in front of Emma Jean and then try to kill her, they were growing more desperate than he thought.

"Do you want me to stay here tonight just in case," Hardy asked her. "I don't mind at all."

Emma Jean smiled at him. "You see that rifle up there on the wall, that was Archie's. He taught me how to use it shortly after we moved here. He said I had to be ready for anything. So, I am good. You go on home and get some rest. You have a bigger fight on your hands than I do."

Hardy made sure all the windows and doors were secure before he left. He got the rifle down and ensured it was good before giving it to Emma Jean. She would be moving slower with her injury, so he wanted her to be as prepared as possible in case they came by after he left. He wanted to stay but couldn't push the envelope with her. She was a tough lady, and he didn't want her to feel like he thought she couldn't fend for herself. She fought off a skinwalker for goodness' sake. She could absolutely handle more than what he had first thought. Hardy walked to the garden. He found that he felt more refreshed and could figure things out while he was there more than anywhere else.

But he found something odd on the gifting stump when he got there. Something he had never seen before. This wasn't an ordinary gift that was usually left for him. It wasn't from the littles nor Luna. What he saw was something he had seen the other night when he had that encounter with what he could only have believed to be a Skinwalker. There, on the stump, lay a strip of what appeared to be white fabric. But it was aged, dirty, tattered, and torn. This came off of the Skinwalker he had seen that night. Was the Skinwalker really dead? This made Hardy question everything. If it weren't dead, did it know about this stump to leave this for him? Hardy was perplexed. He knew he shot it. It appeared he had killed it. Of course, to his credit, it looked like it had died years ago anyway. Was he mistaken all along?

The biggest fear Hardy had was maybe these shifters were the ones who moved the body. They had to have known about this stump. Maybe they're the ones who left this as a way of saying they knew he had shot it. Hardy looked all around his surroundings to be sure he wasn't being followed or watched, picked up the decrepit piece of fabric, and walked home with it clutched in his hand. So many questions were spinning in his mind. This was like some big puzzle, and Hardy knew he was the final piece. He would be the only one who could put all the pieces together and finally destroy it, making this land safe for anyone who inhabited it.

He was glad to see the empty rocker on his front deck. He didn't see anything as unusual as he expected after the ordeal at Emma Jean's cabin. There weren't any signs that the sneaky, shape-shifting ranger had been there. He walked inside and laid the fabric down. He just needed a minute to process everything. This had taken its toll on him and today's events, which had fatigued his mind more than anything else. He was growing weary in dealing with this, but he knew that in due time, it would be over. He lay in bed thinking over everything he had learned and everything that had happened. Before he knew it, he had fallen asleep. He jerked awake sometime after when he heard footsteps walking back and forth across the deck. He grabbed his rifle and slowly crept to the window.

He saw nothing when he carefully moved the curtain back to look out. Was he hearing things that weren't really there? Maybe it was just his imagination. That thought went out the window when he saw his rocking chair start rocking slowly back and forth as if someone were sitting in it. But clearly, there was no one there. Maybe it was the wind. But that thought was also dismissed when he noticed the tree branches weren't moving and his flag by the shed was still. But yet, the rocking chair kept rocking. Soon after, the rocking chair started rocking faster and faster. Hardy was afraid. He had no idea what was going on. Then, a thought entered his mind that terrified him most of all. Spirits. This had to be a ghost. Just as he thought his rocker couldn't go any faster without breaking, the movement stopped. It was once again still.

Hardy didn't know if it was safe to go out or not. You can't see ghosts unless they want you to see them. How do you fight something that you can't see? You can't. He watched his chair periodically for about an hour. It was nearing dusk by then. It hadn't moved a lick since the last time. Having no choice but to believe whatever was out there was now gone, he cautiously opened the door and stepped out. He heard a whistle toward the woods where the ranger walked that day. Utana. He was excited to hear his whistle. It must be safe.

"They're only distractions," He heard a voice say. "Don't let them frighten you. They can't hurt you. They're only here to scare you off. Don't let that happen."

Hardy knew that Utana was speaking by the gruff tone of his

words. But how could he not let something like that scare him? Seeing something like that was terrifying.

"You know the veil is torn. More things will start coming for you, be ready. We have taken care of one of them for you. You will not be held accountable for your action the other night. Luna ensured that the bullet you fired would be the kind you needed to kill the skin-walker, then I moved it from your yard. The strip of fabric I left was for you to know it had been handled."

Hardy didn't know if he could handle anymore himself, so he was thankful for at least that much. It had been too much already. The next day he walked to the water where he did all of his fishing. He sat on the bank, and watched as the slow current pulled the water across the rocks. This is what he had in mind for his retirement.

He climbed up the steeper banks off to the side and trudged through the bramble of brush and vines until he was finally across. He saw the disturbance in the ground and walked over to it. He didn't have anything to dig with, so he just used his hands and a broken branch to get whatever that was unearthed. The more he dug, however, the more confused he became. What could this be? It almost looked like a box. He kept digging deeper and deeper. Finally, he was able to pull it from the ground's grasp. He noted that it was heavy but carried it back around to where he had a more suitable place to sit to try to get into it. Once on the other side, he cleaned the dirt and mud from his hands in the cold water and dried them on his jeans. The white box was beaten up and taped closed. He started wondering if he should even open it at this point. With everything that had already gone on and how this box was taped closed and buried, he thought he should just throw it into the water and let it sink to the depths and be forgotten about.

Generally, if anyone had gone to these lengths to hide something, whatever is in it couldn't be good. But Hardy was curious; now he just had to know what was in it. He tore at the tape until it finally broke loose. He unwound the tape from all over the box and opened it up. It must've been buried there for some time because that smell that escaped from the box when opened was strong and musty. In the box was something in a black trash bag wrapped up. This was getting more unnerving by the second. A box taped closed and buried, that had contents inside that were also wrapped in a black trash bag. Hardy contemplated even harder at that point if he should open it. Someone went to great lengths to hide this for whatever reason.

"Oh well, Hardy said to himself, "Here's goes nothing."

He took the tape off of the outside of the bag. But as he pulled the bag down to reveal what this could be, the sky darkened, and the winds picked up. Hardy paid no mind to it and pulled out what appeared to be a book. A large, hardback book that was very old. He wiped the dust and dirt from the cover and read the title. "The shadow of secrets." As he opened the book, the wind blew its pages ferociously. Thunder echoed through the sky. Hardy put the book back in the bag and carried it and the box home, fearing it would rain. He noted on the way home that the weather was fine. It was only when the book was exposed that things turned dark, and only when the book was opened that it appeared the sky would let loose. Now, however, the sun was shining in the sky, and the sounds of birds could be heard.

He passed the garden, checked the gifting stump for good measure but found nothing new, and walked the rest of the way home. He sat out on the deck, put the box at his feet, and pulled the book from the bag. Again, the sky darkened as he pulled out the book. What was it about this book, and why would it be buried and wound so tightly with tape? He had heard his fair share of stories from the Appalachians but dismissed almost all of them. Now, he had a story all his own. He went inside and decided to see if he could find anything about this book on the internet attached to this property.

He found plenty of stories but none that really stuck out to him concerning the book itself. He did, however, find plenty of stories about seeing several bigfoot and one story about the notorious Skinwalkers. Campers and hikers alike all had their own tales to tell. Some were scarier than others. It was hard to fathom that the stories he read were true. None of the people who wrote them stuck around after their sightings. He didn't blame them honestly.

He took the old Heavy book out, laid it on the table, and opened its cover. The old book cracked as he did so, as if it hadn't been opened in ages. The inscription on the first page read, *"To the holder of this book, continue if you dare. Only read these pages, if you aren't that easy to scare. You will find many spells and secrets inside the pages that will surely blow your mind. Each word you read may come to light; be careful what you read unless you're ready to fight.*

"Peculiar." Hardy thought.

He didn't believe for a second that anything could come to life by simply reading it. In real life, that is, maybe in his mind, but surely not in the present. He continued turning page after page of this mysterious book. Each page held so many interesting things. Stories of the past and what he could only believe to be supposed stories of what the future held. With each turn of the page, the wind seemed to blow harder. But he had to keep going. He was intrigued now and hopeful that maybe something in this book would help him with his venture. Could that be the reason, though, why it was so meticulously wrapped and buried to hopefully never be found again? Who buried it anyway? It was pretty aged, so he could only assume that it had been under the ground for some time.

The next words made him shiver. *"Shapeshifters will come from another dimension, a place of worlds unknown. They'll come from the east to take the land so freely they can roam. No one will know what form they will hold or shape they will take. They could be in the woods in front of your face as a bear, a lion, or a snake. Be on guard as you take this leap so your soul cannot steal. Please heed these words and hold them true, for what is written here is real."*

Thunder cracked loud overhead and made Hardy jump. Just then, a knock at the door. Hardy quickly closed the book and slid it and the box under his bed. He opened the door, and there stood the ranger. He was cautious as he stood eye-to-eye with him. He knew his true form now and was probably one of the shifters that attacked Emma Jean. But he had to play it cool. Even if they knew he was there earlier and knew their secret, he couldn't let on that he did. Hardy walked out onto the deck and noted that the weather had changed again. It was no longer stormy, and the sun was out again.

"What can I do ya for, ranger," Hardy asked slyly. "Is there a problem?"

The ranger looked at Hardy with a smug, perturbed scowl. Hardy could sense the disdain oozing from him and could tell that he was losing his cool with him.

"There was a disturbance a little way from here at the property of Emma Jean Crawford. I wanted to see if you knew anything about it or if she had contacted you." He said, shifting his stance.

Hardy at least had to be honest with him here, for the most part. He knew he could say he didn't, but with everything going on, he had to play the part by being honest a smidge. Continuously lying would only bring more suspicion.

"Yes, sir, I did hear about that." Hardy said.

The ranger almost looked as if he were internally celebrating.

"Did she happen to call you and tell you; how did you find out?"

"Well, I had arranged to go up there because she had some vegetables from the garden she had harvested that she wouldn't be able to eat before they went bad. She didn't want them to go to waste, so I went over to pick them up." Hardy lied.

"I see, I see," the shapeshifting ranger said. "Did she happen to tell you anything of the incident? Maybe what happened to her, who would've done that?"

Hardy sighed. "I walked up to her door and knocked, but she didn't answer, so I went around back. The back door was slightly opened, so I let myself in. I did notice some things were disheveled, but from what she told me when she came out of the back room, she had opened the door because she heard a noise, almost like someone knocking and an animal tore into her house. She did receive some pretty gnarly scratches on her leg from it, but we cleaned it up and put a bandage on it. She was doing okay when I left."

"Did she happen to say what this animal may have been by chance, Hardy?" he asked as he held a notepad as if he were taking notes. "As a park ranger, it's my job to know when these things happen so we can take care of the situation and keep those who live here and visit here safe."

"She didn't. I don't even know if she knew, honestly, but I would have to assume that it was just some wild animal who got spooked, and Emma Jean just caught the brunt end of it." Hardy said, eyeing him.

Suddenly, a low hum came from inside Hardy's house that caught both the ranger's and Hardy's attention. The ranger tried to peer over Hardy's shoulder to look inside. Hardy turned around and looked to see if he could see what it was and noticed a slight glow from under his bed. The book, the humming sound was coming from the book. Hardly turned to face the ranger, walked the rest of the way onto the deck, and closed the door behind him.

"Damn refrigerator, must be on the fritz again." Hardy said.

"Yeah, sure." The ranger said. "Well, I'm going to get out of this heat. It's gotten to be extremely hot, and I need to get back." He said, and he quickly left.

Hardy could tell something was off with him since the hum started. He had a strange look, almost like he was in pain. Hardy followed behind him, keeping his distance. But instantly, the ranger disappeared. This time, however, he made a mistake. In the field where he was walking lay his ranger outfit in a small heap on the ground. Hardy reached down to try to pick it up with a large stick. When he lifted the shirt, a large pile of what appeared to be slime fell out of it with a slimy squish sound as it hit the ground. Hardy quickly dropped the shirt and the stick and backed up slowly. Fear gripped his body. Was this the remnants of the shapeshifter? Had he started to change too soon and hadn't a choice but to leave the clothes behind as he ran away, or worse yet, was this the shifter who seemingly dissolved before he could return to their base?

Hardy had to get back home. He was sure that the answers he needed were in that book. On the way back, he felt confident it came to him at the right time. How else could he explain how he suddenly just stumbled across it that day? It was all falling in line. There are no coincidences, and he couldn't be told otherwise. When he returned home, the book was now lying on the table. Hardy was in shock. He knew it was under his bed, and no one had been there since he took off to follow the ranger. How could it possibly be out of the box under the bed and now lying on the table opened? He walked to the table and sat down. The pages the book was opened to read, *"Once in secret, now exposed, the truth you seek, is behind doors unclosed. Knock, and you shall enter, seek and you shall find. The time is now upon you. Everything's aligned.*

10

Hardy leaned back in his chair, took his glasses off, and laid them on the open pages. He rubbed his face with his callused hands, half wishing, once he opened his eyes again, that he would be back to a time before he moved here. He put his glasses back on and put the box back under his bed. For good measure, though, he also wrapped it back up into the black plastic bag before putting it in the box. The next morning, he showered and grabbed some coffee. He took the box from under his bed and carried it to Emma Jean's. She had to see this. Maybe she would know what was going on.

He was also eager to tell her what happened with the shape-shifting ranger. As he walked to her cabin, there were strange noises that he hadn't ever heard before coming from the woods. Not just snarls and growls now. These were like the sounds of snakes or cat hissing. The sounds were forceful, and the velocity of the sounds almost vibrated his brain.

Although the sound surrounded him, nothing came out of the wood line. It was almost as if he had a shield of protection around him. H made it to Emma Jean's and laid the large, heavy box on her coffee table.

"What do you have there?" Emma Jean asked, eyeing the unopened white box.

Hardy sat down and started opening it. "I happened to see this down at the water where I fish. I caught just a glimpse of the white corner sticking up on the ground on the opposite side. I was curious about what I was seeing so I went over to it and started digging. I unearthed the box and opened it up."

He pulled out the black plastic bag, exposed the aged, tattered book, and laid it on the table. He sat the bag and box on the floor as she got up and slowly made her way to where he sat.

"Wow," Emma Jean said as she looked at the mysterious book. "That certainly has some age to it, doesn't it, Hardy? The Book of Secrets. Pretty intriguing title, huh."

"Yes, ma'am, but even more than that, it has to have some sort of powers or something."

Emma Jean looked at Hardy, shocked at what he had just said. "Powers, Hardy?"

Hardy told her what had happened and how it seemed as if by simply hearing the hum from it, the shape-shifting ranger either changed too quickly to worry about his clothes or the latter...he somehow disintegrated in the field. He showed her in the book how the secrets were now exposed and that everything had aligned.

"I just had to show you to get your take on it. I know you may not know anything about it or what it does, but I did at least want your eyes on it." Hardy said.

"This isn't some sort of witchcraft, is it, Hardy?" Emma Jean asked, concerned.

Hardy hadn't thought of that. He hoped not. He was really wishing he had researched the book further before opening the book now. He placed it back in the black bag and back into the box.

"Maybe that's why the weather turned weird when I opened it at the water or home. Come to think of it, as soon as I read about the shapeshifters, the ranger showed up. Then, on the way here, I heard a very loud, piercing hiss sound coming from the forest as I walked carrying the box. Oh no, what have I done?" Hardy asked as he put his head in his hands.

Hardy wasn't into that anymore than he was trying to be in the middle of what he was already in. He decided to go home right then and see if he could find anything out about the book he had unearthed and brought into his home. If that's what this book was, he had decided to take it straight back and bury it where he found it. After he taped it all back up again, that is. The loud hiss followed him home again after he left Emma Jean's. He just clutched the box tighter and made it home in record time. He left the box on the deck outside, sat down, and researched all he could.

Hardy breathed a sigh of relief. The Book of Secrets wasn't witch-craft, after all. In fact, it wasn't bad intentions for humans at all. According to the article, this book seemed to have stumbled here decades ago. It said a farmer had it and was attempting to use it to get rid of some unruly beasts on his property. Unfortunately, he was unsuccessful and after the wayward animals had their own way with the farmer, the book fell into the hands of someone more sinister. Someone on the darker side, and this person, in turn, wrapped a black bag around it to prohibit its powers of destruction towards the beast and strange entities of the land and then it was buried. After he read that article, nothing else could be found about the book anywhere.

That explained a lot. The ranger showed up after he read about the shapeshifters, then the low-frequency hum that came from the book with the ranger around. After that, seemingly, the ranger either changed and ran off without his clothes or he dissolved right there near Hardy's cabin. Afterward, on the walk to Emma Jean's and back home, he was surrounded by all the strange hissing. But he was never stalked or attacked. They all knew what he had. There's no way they couldn't know. This book was probably here on the property long before Hardy was even born. They may have lived in a different dimen-sion altogether, but they were trying to get here to inhabit this land. But they can't with the book unearthed and in the hands of a clean soul.

Hardy walked outside, grabbed the box, and brought it back in. He unwrapped the plastic bag from around it, laid it on the kitchen table, and just stared at it. If what he thought were true, he would be sure to take this book everywhere he went. This would be his way to stay safe and protected without the brute strength of any soldier or without the firepower from his weapon. Henry grabbed the book and went and sat on the deck in his rocking chair, something he hadn't felt comfortable doing since the night the skinwalker came to the bottom of his stairs. He felt a small pebble hit the leg of his jeans. His face lit up, and he was overwhelmed with joy.

"The littles," Hardy said out loud as he stood up. "The littles have come back!"

Hardy was so excited to play with them once again. They hadn't been by to play since the ranger came over the very first time. I guess the ranger really did dissolve. They came back because they felt safe. He looked down at the book on his rocking chair and smiled. He had all the confidence in the world now. He would have to do more reading, but he knew all the answers would be in the book for him to use to clear the evil off the land for everyone, including the Bigfoot family. Hardy sat outside and played with the little until it was completely dark, and he could hear their footsteps retreating into the woods, followed byhigh-pitched squeals. He went inside with the book and laid it on the kitchen table. He changed and went to bed with a smile on his face.

The next morning, he sat at the table with his cup of coffee and reviewed every page of the book he could take in. He read about the skinwalkers, the dogmen, the dark shadow entities, and the shapeshifters. He moved on to the following chapters and read about the portals and the different dimensions. Acknowledging that there was one portal would be enough for anyone, but reading about how there were more out there was chilling.

He flipped to the back pages, hoping to find an index. He didn't find the index there either, but what he found he thought may help him more. A letter in very neat print. The name was faded at the bottom with age, so he didn't know who wrote it. He wondered if it could be from the farmer based on what it said.

"If you happen to be reading this, it only means that I was unsuccessful in getting the evil out of this place. Some ran, but some stayed. Some also vowed to return. I don't know what my demise was; honestly, it doesn't matter. I just hope that whoever finds this book next takes care of the problem once and for all for themselves and anyone else who follows behind them."

Hardy folded the letter back up and returned it to where he found it in the book. Now, he knew he had to avenge the farmer as well. He would see to it that he did. He felt really good about handling this now that he had something similar to a study guide. Utana kept saying the time was drawing near. But now that the veil was torn and all these things were getting through, he wondered when that time would be. He took the book with him and walked the path the ranger took to where he inevitably dissolved.

He was on the hunt for Utana. They mainly came from this side, so he thought that they all should be around there somewhere. He walked further than he ever had because he had the confidence of the book he carried in his arms. It was heavy, but he would carry it anywhere he had to if it meant he, along with anyone else with him, would be assured their safety.

He found more than Utana. He found every bigfoot on the property it seemed. The littles ran up to greet him first, held onto his pant legs, and walked him in further. There stood Utana right in the middle of a clearing surrounded by tall trees. Utana noticed the book he carried in his arm. He gave Hardy a half-cocked grin. Utana didn't have to say a word. Hardy knew he was pleased that he had found the book.

"Now," Utana said, "Now we begin."

Hardy sat with all of the bigfoot, amazed. He couldn't believe that he was even getting to experience this. Despite all he had been through in just a few short months, it was still all so surreal. The wind blew cold against his skin just then. Fall was upon them. He had brushed off that fact with things going on as they have. To him, anytime the sun was out, it was too warm on his skin. He was a fan of fall. He first moved here in the summer months and was glad there was some reprieve from the heat. He wondered how the bigfoot dealt with the cold. Could they build fires as well, just like humans, or did they stay in caves? There had to be some way. He was sure he would find out living this close to them and being accepted into their family group.

Utana motioned for him to sit down. Laying the book on the ground, Hardy sat on a large boulder. Although friends, he still felt a little uncomfortable about the new bigfoot he had just met. Some were tall and thin, and some were broad and thick. There were both male and female alike surrounding him. One of the littles came over to him and held his hand. That made Hardy feel better. Maybe this little could sense his unease.

A small female voice whispered in his ear. "You have done a good thing by finding that book. It will heal this land of all evil forever. It was taken decades ago by an evil entity that harassed every good being that inhabits this place. He will be the one you need to destroy before our land is doomed for all eternity."

Hardy looked down at the little. The face of innocence. It knows no evil currently. It wasn't corrupted in any way. The eyes are said to be the window to the soul, and this little soul was pure. He was going to do his best to ensure it stayed that way. Hardy didn't really feel comfortable using telepathy to talk yet. He was always startled when he heard a voice that wasn't his own. He honestly, still felt a little crazy when that happened.

"I think this book senses when evil is around, and I know they sense when I have this book," Hardy said. "When the ranger came by, the book hummed, but when he left, he dissolved, almost like he melted. When I took it to Emma Jean's cabin, the woods were surrounded by hissing when I walked through there. I know this book has powers, so I never go anywhere without it now. I feel safe with it in my hands."

Utana gruffed. "And safe you are, Hardy, as long as you have that book and don't let them take possession of it, we all are. No harm will come to any good thing as long as a pure soul has it. I knew the farmer. He walked outside without the book. The dogmen tore him apart. They took advantage of the fact he wasn't protected, and that was it. They have only been toying with you up until now. But rest assured, the games are over now. You have the book. The ranger was the beginning, and now that he's gone, they will all be working against you even more. Don't leave without that book."

Hard was confused by Utana's statement. He knew the farmer. How could he have known the farmer? All this happened with the farmer a long, long time ago. Exactly how old was Utana anyway was the question.

He would have to be over one hundred years old. No wonder he was getting tired. He assumed that one of the other male bigfoot standing around him would take over after Utana. He scanned their faces, wondering who it would be and how the hierarchy fell in the bigfoot realm. Even if he knew, he probably still wouldn't understand.

"So, "Hardy began, "He walked outside without the book, and they attacked him. Why haven't they done that to me before I had the book?"

"You weren't a true threat then. You were only seen as an inconvenience. But now that you have unearthed that book, they know you hold the power to erase them for good. They have merely been trying to scare you off so you wouldn't find it. Now that you hold that book, you also hold the target that comes with it. Now, if you leave your property without it, you no longer have any protection. You've read all of what's in there, I take it?" Utana asked.

"I've read through some of it. Just enough to get a feel for what's here. That's when I flipped to the back of the book and found the note from the farmer." Hardy replied.

"I see, Utana said. "I suggest you take this home and read through all of it. That way, you are truly empowered with all the knowledge and power the book holds. That will prepare you. You will need it. My best advice, however, is do not be afraid. These beings feed off of fear. It only makes them more powerful. The more confident you are, the better off you'll be."

Hardy wasn't sure if he could do that. He had plenty of incidences in the field as an officer that he could handle confidently, but others scared him. Even though he had a gun and a badge, under that, he was still a human being with feelings and emotions. Seeing the rocking chair being rocked back and forth scared him. How much more would seeing dark beings, dog men, and goodness only knows what else coming for him scare him? How could he not be? He took Utana's advice back home with him that day. He was sure to leave the book lying on his kitchen table that night as he went to sleep. First, he would open the book and start down the road to bringing peace again back to these woods.

Howls woke Hardy in the middle of the night. The book opened almost as if someone were sitting at the table and turned its cover. Hardy walked over to the table and sat down. He glanced at his watch. Seeing as how it was only a little after two in the morning, he wouldn't be tempted to read it now. He needed rest. He closed the cover and laid back down. He fell asleep as he heard everything was silent once again. That would be short-lived, however. Not too long afterward, a loud screech called out and woke him again. The book once again opened. Hardy was tired and frustrated. He just wanted to sleep. His body ached for it. He got up and sat at the table. What is going on with this damn book? He closed the cover again and went back to bed. This time, he pulled his covers over his head to block out any noises. Hardy just needed a break to take it all in. He wouldn't be able to do anything if he were that tired. The next thing Hardy knew, it was morning. Seven thirty, and the birds were beginning to sing. He was glad to hear something natural and normal for once. From what he read in this book, there are things in these woods that he hasn't even experienced yet.

Things he didn't want to experience. But when would he, would it all be at the same time, would he have time to prepare, or worse yet, would they devour him? He decided to walk to the water to clear his mind. The light trickle from the water relaxed him, and he decided to take his phone this time and play his meditation music as well. While he sat in the grass looking out across the water and reading his paperback book, a flinting glimpse of something larger flew by. He was afraid that it was a large bee or something else that would sting him. He looked all around him and didn't see it anymore.

He went on reading and didn't give it another thought...until it came back. He swatted at it with his book, hoping that even if he didn't hit it, it would at least take a hint to leave him alone. It was more irritating than anything when it flew at him again. He smacked it with the book this time and flung it back into the woods. But then, something that would only happen in the movies came to life. Out of the woods walked a faerie. Not to be mistaken with your traditional fairies. He read about the faerie (or Fae) as it is called in the book just that morning. These are the more mischievous and carry more malevolent intent.

He noted how the faerie looked. He felt as if he were looking at a child. He had on clothes that looked like he was from a different time. They were definitely not relevant to these days. His ears came to a point, and he had speckled cheeks. Hardy had to sit back down in fear he would pass out. Did they hear his thoughts? He asked the question in his mind of when he would experience things he hadn't seen yet, and here he was, looking at a faerie that he had read about.

"What's your problem, mister?" the faerie said in an irritated tone as he straightened out his clothes. "Are you trying to kill me?"

Hardy was speechless. Was this faerie the bug that was just flying in his face? It shape shifted. No longer small enough to swat, he stood in front of him as a human. Albeit, he was a different-looking human than he had ever seen before.

"You're a faerie." Hardy finally managed to say.

"Ahh, good for you, you know your sprites." The faerie said.

"You look nothing like Tinkerbelle, though." Hardy said.

The faerie fell to the ground, laughing heartily. "You're kidding me, right, me, look like that fruitcake? I'm not that kind of fairy. Different faerie altogether there, bud." He continued as he stood back up, still laughing.

11

Hardy only knew of the friendly little fairy in Peter Pan named Tinkerbelle. No doubt, this one was different. He didn't seem nice at all. That didn't surprise Hardy. Not much in these woods were nice that he came across. Just then, the pages to the book flew open. Hardy looked at the faerie and then back at the book. The faerie gave him a smug look and took off into the woods. He walked over to the book. He had no clue what that interaction with the faerie was all about, but he was sure that it couldn't have been good since the book opened as the faerie drew closer to Hardy. He sat back down and lifted the open book onto his lap and read what it said.

"Though small in nature, they are trite. Keep your distance from these menacing sprites. Malice and evil, they bring to your day. They're not friendly. They're part of the fae. A different faerie than you read of in books. Don't be fooled by their minuscule looks. A distraction to most for something bigger that's planned, if you've seen them already, you're in their hand."

Hardy wasn't too sure what to make of that, but he knew he was ready to finally be done with all this mess. He picked up the paperback he was reading as well as the big book he had found and walked back home. Whispers echoed out of the forest all around him. It was like actual people were nestled in the woods having a hushed conversation. But this sound didn't come from just a few people. This sounded like a room full of thousands, all whispering in unison. He felt like eyes were staring at him as he walked home. This was the most uncomfortable walk home he had taken since moving there. He knew it was because of the book he was carrying, and although relieved for the protection, he just wanted to get it home and out of his hands.

He had just about made it home when it sounded like a freight train was rushing toward him through the trees. All at once, the birds went silent, and the whispers ceased. A loud growl pierced the silence, and an evil voice then echoed from the tree line.

"You think you have won because of the book that you hold in your hands? You are sadly mistaken. You will be cared for just like the farmer who held it before you. You will get careless just the same, and I will be waiting. No book can protect you forever. You are mine!" The evil voice boomed.

Hardy ran the rest of the way home. He was shaking, and he was scared. They acknowledged him. Whatever this evil was spoke to him. He started losing his confidence after that. Self-doubt crept back in. There was no way he was any match to whatever held that booming voice. He would be mincemeat in no time. The book opened once again. Hardy rolled his eyes. He wasn't ready for anything the book had to say. He just wanted to pack up his clothes and belongings that he could carry and leave this place behind. But then he thought of Emma Jean, the bigfoot family, the littles. He couldn't do that, and he was so damn frustrated. But it was a fact. He, for whatever reason, was seen fit to be chosen to heal this land. But what he had just experienced shook him to his core.

He decided to read what the book was wanting to tell him. He still didn't understand how this book knew everything. After all of his experiences, that book had something to say. Couldn't it, for once, tell him to just leave? Hardy chuckled at that, but he knew it was impossible. Could he leave? Sure, he could. But it would be certain death for all who remained, and he just couldn't do that to his friends because of the fear and doubt that he carried. He walked over to the book on the table and sat down, prepared for whatever this thing had to tell him.

"The master of the land is evil and strong. He wishes to cast out all who don't belong, a land of villains he wants to proclaim, for an eternity to rule, an eternity to reign. You must not doubt in your steady powers, but he is coming for you now; be ever on the ready."

"Oh, brother," Hardy sighed. "Well, this should be fun."

He decided to read further into the book. It had something to say about everything he was experiencing at the time, but he was sure that when he would sit and read it as he was now, none of this would show up in the book. When Hardy read it, it was only information about the spirits and evil he would experience. But anytime something happened, the book would open itself to reveal something he hadn't ever run across when he read it alone.

Maybe that's why it was called the book of secrets. What it held was secret until the time it was needed. What it held was secret until the time it was needed. He began reading the information listed as "The Lamashtu." This was said in the book to be one of the most evil entities inhabiting the land that Hardy now called home. This being, or spirit, almost resembles that of a dogman. Carrying the same characteristics with pointed ears, long snout, sinister eyes, and heinous acts. The name itself means, "The one who erases." Hardy shivered at that. He had a feeling that the voice he heard in the woods came from this spirit or demoness as it is known to be.

It is said to have come from the Mesopotamian religion and is known worldwide as the most terrible of all female demons.

Hardy would have to be extremely careful with this demon in the woods. Not only was she out to annihilate him off the land, but he also read that she was a master of trickery. He went on to read about how she could perform illusions and disguise herself or specific objects.

"Great," Hardy thought. "I'm going to be looking for something as phony as a raisin cookie in a bowl full of chocolate chip cookies. Just something else to blow any trust I have out of the window for anything."

Hardy thought back to the faerie he had seen earlier in the day. He knew the book had said it was a sprite, but after reading what he had just read, what if the sprite was really this crazy dog man being in disguise? Now, he would have to question everything, all the while, keeping enough wits about him to know the difference. Hardy walked outside to sit on his deck. The weather was growing colder but still just warm enough for him to enjoy without being overly hot. He brought the book with him and laid it at his feet off to the side. He heard rustling in the bushes just then. He tried to not be afraid. He knew that his fear would feed whatever was out there, and having the book or not, Hardy wasn't trying to do anything to strengthen them.

He leaned over and looked at the bushes and trees where the bigfoot usually come from, but the vegetation was rustling from the opposite side. Just then, out of the tall grasses, a small, hairy, pot belly animal walked out into the open. This thing looked like one of the littles, but something just didn't seem right. Was it an offshoot of bigfoot? Was that a thing? It looked pleasant enough and didn't have any scary features. Hardy smiled at it and waved.

"How are you, little fella?" he said as he stood and walked towards it.

It just stood looking at him. It didn't return his greeting or run up to him and grab his pant legs as the littles did. He assumed it must just be shy.

"You don't have to be scared; I won't hurt you. I'm a nice man. Do you want to play?" Hardy asked, trying to gain its trust.

Still, yet, this small, shaggy creature just stared at him. Finally, after a little while, it held out its hand for Hardy. Hardy stood up and began walking down his deck stairs to where it stood. It acted like it wanted him to follow him. With each step he took down the stairs to go over to this creature, the wind blew, and the sky grew darker. Hardy stopped and looked around as he noticed the change in the weather. He knew that generally, that quick of a change was when the book was opened. When Hardy had reached the last step and was putting his foot down on the grass to walk over to this thing, a voice rang out loud in his ears.

"No, Hardy, don't go any further!" It was Utana.

The small shaggy being acted almost as if it had also heard Utana's voice. It took off back into the trees, and before Hardy could blink, it was gone.

Utana walked out from behind one of the tall trees beside Hardy's cabin.

"That wasn't one of us. That was a creature known as the puckwudgie. Another shapeshifter, if you will. Once nice, now mean. They will lore you in, tricking you into thinking they are nice. Then, once they have you where they want you, they will harm you or, worse yet, kill you. You have to be more careful, Hardy. Not to mention, this thing tricked you into leaving the book on the deck. You are fair game once you no longer have that book near you. You are then the prey. Believe me, you will not win against these."

Hardy felt like a fool. He was embarrassed that he had let that happen. He was tempted to not even leave the cabin again in fear that these tricksters would fool him again.

"I'm sorry, Utana. I was tricked, but I honestly thought it was one of the little ones, but I did sense something was off about it. I thought it was just shy. But like the littles, I didn't want it to feel alone or afraid of me. I wanted it to know I was a nice man."

"You were almost a dead man, Hardy." Utana said sternly.

Hardy hung his head. "Yeah, I know. I'll be more careful, I promise."

Utana backed up into the trees and disappeared. Hardy grabbed the book and walked inside. They can only get him if he doesn't have the book with him. That's why this puckwudgie had tried to get him away from it. He was almost successful as well. Hardy was thankful that Utana had been watching out for him. He knew he would've walked all the way over to it and been gone. Then, everything and everyone who lived here would be doomed. Hardy decided that he now needed to be more tactful. He wanted to get a feel for what was going on at home and when he wasn't watching.

He went into his shed and grabbed a couple of trail cams. Now that he had become friends with this bigfoot family, and most importantly, Utana, he felt comfortable putting them out again with Utana, knowing that he didn't mean any ill intent. He was hopeful that when Utana saw them this time, he wouldn't take them down and throw them. He never did find the first one he had put up. He certainly wasn't going to be looking for that anymore since all this was happening.

He strapped one to the tree on either side of his cabin and then one directly in front of his cabin, facing his front door. That way, he had a 360 view, except for behind his cabin. Nothing would be able to get by him. He hoped anyway. With night falling, he fumbled to pick up the book to walk back in when he heard a loud call from behind him. He turned around and stood as still as possible so he didn't make a noise. He didn't even take a breath. All was silent once again. He scurried inside just as the sun went down.

"Whatever that was," Hardy said out loud, "These cameras should pick it up."

He kept the book close by when he went in. He was beginning to feel like this book was similar to a dog's. He never left home without it. It stayed near him when he slept. The only difference is that he didn't have to feed it or take it outside to go to the bathroom. He even takes the damn thing for walks. He laid the book down on the kitchen table and went to bed. He didn't hear anything disturbing throughout the night, and he was a little discouraged. Maybe the trail cams kept things at bay. He had always heard that, that happened anytime you put them up.

Nonetheless, he walked outside with his trusty book in his arms to check the trail cam footage. He saw nothing on the sd cards from the trail cams by his house. However, the trail cam facing his cabin had something he couldn't believe. He took the SD card and the laptop inside. He couldn't be sure, but he was afraid that what he saw might have been the sun's reflection on the screen. He played through the footage again, but it wasn't a glare. Timestamped at around two o'clock in the morning, he saw apparitions. Ghostly figures seemed to be floating a few feet off the ground as if they were walking, but clearly, they weren't. There were at least five of them.

With blank stares, they made their way around his property with no real destination and with none of them interacting with one another. Then, at around two-thirty, they all just suddenly vanished as if they weren't there to begin with. Hardy sped through the other pictures taken and saw nothing. He knew that soon, the battle would begin. Hardy sped through the other pictures taken and saw nothing. He knew that soon, the battle would begin. Hardy walked back outside and put the SD card back into the trail cam after saving the photos to his laptop. He got a cold chill when he walked where he knew the apparitions had been. Things were ramping up and getting more curious.

He decided to walk to his farm while he was out. He needed to get the rest of the vegetables harvested before the cold snap hit, and they wouldn't be any good. As he got closer, he saw something standing next to it. Just a shape at first. He couldn't quite make it out, and he was trying to reason what it was. To Hardy's surprise, as he got closer, he saw that it was a deer.

"Well," Hardy said aloud, "Would you look at that, something that actually belongs in these woods and not something supernatural trying to kill me for once."

He slowly approached it, not wanting to scare it. He didn't mind if the deer ate some of his vegetables. Truth be told, he wouldn't be able to gather them all. Even if he could, they would surely go bad before he could eat them. He was surprised the deer didn't run off the closer he got.

"You must be pretty hungry not to run off, girl." He said as he approached the doe.

She was standing there staring at him while she chewed. Each of her ears turning from side to side like beacons so she could run if she heard something. But she just stood with Hardy. No fear in her at all and no cause for alarm prompting her to run. He was surprised at that. Not really typical deer behavior but he would take it. She suddenly froze and looked into the woods. Hardy looked in the direction she was, but he didn't see or hear anything at all.

Something definitely spooked her though. She stood motionless for a while just staring out into the dense vegetation. With a sudden burst of energy, she took off running into the thick brush and was gone.

Hardy just shook his head, got what he came for, and returned to the cabin. He made his way in, got all of his stuff taken care of and put away and sat on the deck and started reading his paperback book. The silence was broken by the ringing of his cell phone from inside. Hardy thought it could be another shape-shifting ranger and had debated not getting up to answer it. But it just kept ringing. He put his book face down in his rocker and walked inside to get it.

He was surprised to see who it actually was.

"Emma Jean, what a nice surprise," Hardy said, smiling. "How are you doing?"

Silence echoed on the other end of the phone. Not one single peep could be heard. He had thought she called by accident. Maybe she didn't even know that she had called him. After repeating her name several times and getting no reply, Hardy hung up. About thirty minutes passed by, and his cell phone rang again. He was kicking himself for just not bringing it back out here with him, but to be honest, he despised those things.

Once again, he let it go. But the second set of rings piqued his curiosity. He put his book down as before and walked inside to answer his phone. This time, it wasn't Emma Jean. It was an unknown number. He typically didn't answer those at all, but with its continuous back-to-back calling, he thought it might be important. But again, he was still met with the same silence upon answering. He hung up after saying hello several times and getting nothing in reply. This time, he set his phone to vibrate before he slid his cell phone into his pocket and walked outside to finish his book.

His phone vibrated in his pocket. Hardy was growing quite perturbed at this point. He pulled his phone out of his pocket and was going to just turn it off. However, he saw Emma Jean's name on the phone and answered it again.

"Emma Jean," Hardy said as he answered his phone. "Are you messing with me?"

This time, he wasn't met with silence.

"Hardy, they're here. They're creeping around my property, circling my cabin. I can hear them snarling and growling. I'm afraid, please, please come help me."

Just then, the call dropped, and silence was, once again, all he heard. Hardy swiftly grabbed his rifle, the book of secrets, and he shoved his cell phone back in his pocket just in case she called again. As he ran to Emma Jean's, the sky grew dark and the whistling of the wind echoed through the trees. Hardy felt this uncomfortable presence around him, but he didn't let it deter him from getting to his friend. He hadn't ever heard that side of Emma Jean before. She was always so confident when she spoke. Even after her attack that day, she still sounded the same. He didn't think she had a meek bone in her body. But the voice he heard on the other end of the phone reminded him of talking to a child who'd had a nightmare.

Laughter then encircled him as he ran. Low, maniacal laughter. He stopped and looked around him.

"You fool," a growling voice rang through the trees. "You are so easy to break down. You are no match for me. I will win, and I will break you in half. This land will be mine, and you will only be a memory for those who remain."

Hardy's heart was racing.

"Who are you?" he yelled into the trees. "Why don't you show yourself?"

The wind had gone silent and had ceased to blow. He noticed then that everything had gone silent. His phone started vibrating in his pocket. He reached in and grabbed it and saw Emma Jean's name on the screen.

"Emma Jean, I'm coming, I promise. I'm nearly there. Just hang tight." He said.

But he wasn't met with Emma Jean's voice at all. He was again met with the laughter he had just heard bouncing off the trees.

Hardy shook. "What was going on?"

12

Hardy was so upside down with everything that he didn't know what was real. He even considered turning back around and going home. It was obviously just this she-devil messing with him...or was it. After a bit, he decided just to keep going. If he went home, he would just be driving himself crazy trying to figure out if Emma Jean was really okay. If he called her, the legitimacy of the call, would still fall into question. However, he knew without a doubt that laying his eyes on her couldn't be mistaken...he hoped.

His phone vibrated in his pocket as he made his way to Emma Jean's. He didn't even take it out to look and see who it was. In his mind, it wasn't real anyway. He wanted to take it out and fling it into the woods, but he thought better of it.

Once he arrived, he found Emma Jean rocking in her rocking chair on the front deck. She was absolutely fine. Not a thing wrong with her. He felt so much better about that and was glad he had decided to come here. She noticed him and gave him a big smile and waved. After talking with her a bit, he felt confident that it was her and not some shapeshifter.

"Emma Jean, I don't know what's real and what isn't anymore." Hardy began. "It was your voice. I would've bet my life on it, but in reality, it wasn't. This thing is very tricky, and I can almost guarantee that the farmer who fell victim to it was tricked in the same way. I was even mistaken about the littles. I was determined it was a toddler bigfoot. I was wrong. They almost had me. I'm glad that Utana stepped in and saved me. I was so embarrassed, but it wasn't until then that I knew how devious they could be. Then, when they pretended to be you, it made it even worse."

He saw Emma Jean soften her gaze at him. He really didn't want her to feel bad for him. He wasn't looking for pity, but clarity. He knew the attacks were strengthening and would only grow stronger from this point on. He needed the book to tell him what to do. The unfortunate part, however, is that something bad or strange had to happen for it to reveal its secrets. Maybe a new creature would emerge. He was kind of surprised that what happened with what he could only believe to be the Lamashtu didn't prompt the book to open. It didn't even budge. He was afraid to even think of what could be coming.

After ensuring Emma Jean was safe and talking to her for some time, he stood up to go. They had agreed that they needed a secret way to communicate. That way, he would know if it was truly her. She would call once, hang up, and wait five minutes before calling back. That would at least solidify that he was actually talking to her. He agreed to do the same if he called her.

He wanted so desperately to just have a normal life here. He knew that with everything gone, he would be able to have that. Everything festered in him at that moment. He began feeling more confident than he ever had before. He stood on the stump and yelled through the trees.

"Show yourselves, all who inhabit this place. You want a piece of me. Here I am. I am so sick of you toying with me. Let's get this over with. I am ready to be done with all of you!" Hardy yelled.

The woods were silent as a small whisp of wind circled him. No noises, no voices, and no evil came to confront him. That disheartened him. They were all-powerful, but on their terms only. When they're called out, however, they do nothing. But he knew they wouldn't dare do anything to him as long as he had the book. He hopped down from the stump and walked back to his cabin. He sat down again to read the book, hoping it would tell him something; anything. After hours of scouring through the book, he felt sure he had read enough about these entities to have something come for him.

He wanted this to be over, and he knew that generally, when he read of something, it came to pass. So, he did his part to be sure they all came. He read about Skinwalkers, dogmen, the fae, the puckwudgies he had experienced earlier, and several other, not-so-nice beings. He even read of the apparitions he saw on his trail camera that were said to be the souls of all who lived on that land.

He was just waiting for something to happen now. He didn't know when or what, but he knew something eventually would. Several hours passed, and nothing had taken place. He checked out his windows a few times but didn't see or hear anything unusual. Hardy decided to make dinner, shower, and just turn in early. It was frustrating to wait for the inevitable to happen and no way to speed it up, even when he tried. He was growing restless at this point.

A scream echoed, nearly shaking the windows out of Hardy's cabin. Hardy woke with a jolt, instantly panicked by how loud it was and how close it sounded to be. He read about the shrill, soul-shattering scream in the book earlier.

It could only be attributed to the banshee of the woods. He didn't really understand why there would be a banshee in these woods. They're of Irish folklore, but nonetheless, it was here from another dimension, and it had definitely let its presence be known.

Hardy thought as he sat in his bed, afraid to move, that maybe they hadn't come when he called them out, because they had left the area and gone back through an open portal. Maybe there were always different creatures and beings here. Perhaps it wasn't all the same. That would explain the puckwudgie, the banshee, along with the faerie. Prior to them, it had only been things that were said to be normal for that region.

Bigfoot, dogmen, Skinwalkers, other shapeshifters. But now, there were others that he thought didn't really belong in these mountains. Maybe they're only portal jumpers going from one dimension to the next, wreaking havoc in all they enter into.

Either way, they were here, even on occasion, and they would have to be eradicated all the same. It would be in their favor to venture into a different dimension before it's too late.

Hardy caught a glimpse of shadows through his curtains moving around. Anxiety overtook him, and he was even more afraid to come off the bed. Then, he saw the glow from flashlights moving.

Were they truly flashlights, or were they orbs glowing and only appearing to look like flashlights through the cover of his curtains. He didn't know. He fought his intuition to stay in the bed. He had to know if someone was on his property. He slowly swung his shaking legs over the edge of his bed and carefully slid on his house shoes. He tip-toed quietly to the window. He was thankful he had gone with the sheer curtains. He wouldn't have to open them to see out. There were shadows. This wasn't orbs he was seeing. These were people. He walked and grabbed his rifle. Fear was gone; he would not have any person on his property. He threw open the door and held up his rifle.

"You freeze right there, don't take one more step." Hardy said as he pointed his gun at them. "Who are you, and why are you on my property in the middle of the night?"

His adrenaline was high, and he was angry. He had enough on his property without throwing trespassers into the mix.

"We're sorry, mister." One of the young men spoke up. "We weren't going to mess anything up. We were just scared. Our campsite is about two miles back, and we heard strange sounds all around us and saw a tall, dark figure. We ran until we came up to your camp. We were looking for something to protect ourselves with."

Hardy almost felt bad having pulled his gun on them now. They were clearly shaken up.

"Our mom is still at camp; we just need something to take back to protect her." The other young man said.

They didn't appear to be any older than sixteen. Hardy walked off his deck to meet the boys, where they stood by the picnic table. When his flashlight crested their faces, he saw it. Their eyes were completely black.

"These are black-eyed children." He thought to himself.

"Can we come inside your cabin, mister? We won't stay long. We're just scared." The first young man said.

Hardy had already started walking slowly backward away from them, having learned who they actually were. He knew that they couldn't come in without permission.

"No, you do not have my permission to come into my cabin. You do, however, have my permission to get the heck out of here, though." Hardy said as he once again pointed his rifle at them.

"Awe, what's wrong, Hardy? Don't you want to play with us?" they both asked in unison in an evil, demonic tone.

Then, Hardy realized he didn't have the book with him. It was on the table in the kitchen. He wasn't protected. He had to get back inside and quickly.

He watched their faces morph into hideous creatures, and their eyes grew wide, still completely pitch black. They gave chase and nearly had him. He slammed the door in their faces and locked it. For safe measure, he pulled the couch with all his might and put it in front of the door. They pounded on the door for a while. Hardy had contemplated shooting them through the door, but he didn't figure it would harm them, and it would only ruin his front door in the process. He eventually fell asleep on the couch after the banging finally stopped. He woke as the dawn light came streaming through the curtains, hitting him in the face.

He looked around, taken off guard that he wasn't in his bed, and he haphazardly rolled off the couch. He stood up, peeked out his window but saw nothing, and went to the kitchen. After he had all of his morning's amenities, he sat down. He glanced over to the side of the table and realized his book was opened. Had it been that way all night, or was it like that when he ran in the door and just didn't realize it?

He pulled the book over to him gently by its open cover and read what the words said sprawled across its open pages.

"They come at night to seek your help. In sweet voices, they proclaim, only then, to swindle you, to enter your domain. They are not those whom they portray. Their evil lies within, with dark black eyes, they beckon you in hopes that they will win. Don't be fooled or find compassion for these wicked souls. Once allowed in the place you dwell, they'll surely swallow you whole.

Hardy had read about the black-eyed children in the book. He also read where they don't only show up as children but adults as well. The main form they take is children, however, seeing as how most people will have a soft spot for kids more so than adults. They will be more likely to offer help or allow them to come in where they are and feel safe. It only took Hardy seeing their eyes to know what the teenagers actually were. He wouldn't be swindled. The echo of their evil voices still rang through his ears.

They knew him. They said his name. He remembered everything he had read and could only wait for whatever would come next. Hardy knew, though, that he would have to be more vigilant. That was the second time he has been tricked to come away from the protection that the book holds for him. First with the puckwudgie and now the black-eyed kids.

Utana would surely string him up if the reason that everything failed was because of his own carelessness. He was the chosen one, the one to put an end to it all. Hardy sat on his deck, just eyeing his property with the book securely on his lap. This thing wouldn't be away from him from now on. He would even take it with him to the bathroom at this point. Just then, Utana walked out from the side of the house and got Hardy's attention by giving a slight whistle. He stood up and walked down into the bushes to meet him.

Utana had him follow him to the tree, where Hardy met all of the bigfoot family. Luna was there and ushered Hardy to sit down. He was confused. What could this be about? Did Utana know about last night and the black-eyed teens that came? Did he know about him leaving the book inside when he walked outside?

A little came up and climbed on his lap. Hardy enjoyed the fact that they were so taken by him. They had such a big heart for him.

Luna carried purple flowers over to Hardy along with a pestle and mortar dish. He saw something white already in the bottom of the vessel but wasn't sure what it was. She carefully put the purple flowers in and started using the pestle to crush the flowers into some concoction. Once it was combined, she took small leaves from a tree and began putting them all over Hardy's face. He instinctively lurched backwards when she came over for the first application but heard a voice telling him that it's okay. This is an added source of protection and to trust them.

As the concoction was applied, the skies grumbled almost in displeasure. The wind picked up, and the little held on tighter to Hardy in fear. He wrapped his arms around the little, ensuring it that all was fine. While Luna was putting this on his face, neck, and hands, Hardy was almost transported back to a time in his childhood.

He was a young boy playing on his grandparents' farm. The wind was light, and the sun was warm. He walked with his grandpa, picking vegetables and learning everything he had to teach him. Then, he was sitting at the table eating dinner with them. A tear rolled down his cheek. He missed them immensely. It was so real, he could almost smell the large amount of food that sat on his plate in front of him. The peace that came over was almost too much for him to bear. A loud crack of thunder brought him back to reality. Luna had walked over with a vessel made of wood that Kaya undoubtedly carved for this occasion. Luna dipped a small limb of leaves into what he could only assume to be water and sprinkled it on his head.

Hardy didn't understand how any of this would work to protect him, but he was thankful for it all the same. He would take all they could give him. Off to the side, he saw another juvenile about Kaya's age rubbing sticks together to make a fire. He was impressed. They really do know how to make fire. That explains how they stay warm in the winter. Then, if they also go into caves and make fires, they'll be even warmer. Utana walked over to the bigfoot carrying something that looked like a plain stick. He lit the end and walked to Hardy. Utana then went along the outline of Hardy's body, letting the smoke envelop him. This didn't smell like just smoke, though. It had to have been some sort of incense. Its smell was light, like a soft vanilla, but it was pleasant.

As he hovered it around him, Utana sounded like he was saying a prayer. He couldn't understand what he was saying, but it had a rhythmic flow. Afterward, much to Hardy's surprise, Utana leaned down and hugged him. Hardy didn't take a breath. He just wrapped his arms around him as much as he could and returned the embrace. When Utana stood back up, Hardy could see a tear in his eye. People really don't understand these creatures. He couldn't lie, he didn't either. But he could verify now that they weren't too different than other humans. He was sure that there were bad ones out there. But there are also bad humans out there as well. These bigfoot were now Hardy's family.

After what Hardy could only assume to be a protection ceremony was over, Luna, too, hugged Hardy. She was large, but she still had the fragile frame of a typical human female. The little hopped down after it was over, ran over to the others, and started playing. Hardy smiled as he watched them all. Utana had him stand up. All of the bigfoot encircled him, except for the littles. They all joined hands. The skies roared with thunder, and lightning streaked across the sky. Just then, above their heads, a small shimmering portal opened.

"It's time, Hardy. We've done all for you that we can. The rest is now up to you." Utana said.

"What if I mess up? Then we're all doomed." Hardy said as his self-doubt crept back in.

Luna sighed. "The book will tell you what to do."

Hardy chuckled. "With all due respect, Luna, I hardly think that while I'm being attacked, I'll have time to stop and read the pages of that book."

"The book will tell you." Utana repeated.

Hardy conceded. He certainly wasn't going to stand and argue his point with them. He assumed he would just wing it if necessary. As he returned to his cabin, he noted that the portal had disappeared. His next question was, what came through that portal when it opened. The winds were ferociously blowing by the time he made it back home. The air had a different feel to it, almost a different smell to it as well. He laid the book on the table, and it instantly opened after he laid it down.

"The time is now, you have all you need. It's time to heal this land, we plead. You're our hope to end this fight and set all that's wrong, once again right. They'll come for you, but do not fear, you won't be alone, I'll be here."

That was the second time Hardy was told that. What does this book and Luna think he is going to be able to do?

"It's not like I can just throw my hands in the air and ask the evil creatures for a time-out so I can read this book." He laughed.

Just then, the book began to shake violently. It flew off the table and hit the wall in an instant, falling with a hard thud to the floor. The letter the farmer left in the back of the book floated through the air. The book fell, opened perfectly to the middle pages, and a bright light emerged straight from its center. Hardy had seen a lot of things in his life. He had seen a lot more since moving here. But this, this would be what takes the cake. It was a glowing light, unlike anything he had seen before. It was white with a blue tint to it. Suddenly, something began to form above the light. It appeared to be human in form and stature, but that was impossible.

What wasn't impossible was what he heard.

13

"*H*ardy, I am here to help you fight this battle. We are all depending on you. The ceremony is complete, and the portal is opening in various places throughout this wood spitting out evil beings. The one in which you have to fight is lurking somewhere in between.*"

Her voice was melodic, soothing almost. He no longer felt alone with another person with him. Well, what he could only deem to be human in his mind, even though he knew that wasn't the case.

"You're the voice of the book?" Hardy questioned.

The glowing female entity smiled. "That I am, and I am glad that you have counted yourself all worthy enough to see me as well as hear me. Many have tried, and many have failed. But you, Hardy, are of the purest in spirit. Utana was right to have chosen you."

Hardy wished he felt the same as everyone else. He was growing more uncertain of himself and his abilities. The ceremony conducted by the bigfoot did help him, though. But Hardy didn't have time to think or doubt himself any longer when the sounds of the winds picked up and thunder roared overhead.

"*It's time." The sparkling entity said quietly as she looked out the window. "It's here.*"

"It's here? What's here?" Hardy said out loud.

The door swung open by the force of the wind, almost as if it were going to show Hardy exactly what was outside. Hardy glanced at the book and walked over to pick it up. He was terrified to walk out of the front door but conceded with a small prompt from the hovering entity from the book. But he was not prepared for what he saw when he stepped onto his deck. Many dark figures were flying through the air, cackling that hideous laughter, almost mockingly. The apparitions he had seen on his trail camera were hovering a few feet above the ground, still holding the same oblivious stare. Loud growls could be heard just in the distance, and he saw more rangers. He knew they were shapeshifters. They had all come out of the portal in the sky, still opened. Hardy wondered if there was a way to close it so no more evil could fall from the sky.

"The bigfoot kept telling me you would tell me what to do. I'd say it's high time you got to talking, ma'am." Hardy said to the book entity as he continuously looked around.

"Once entombed in their own dimension, their own skies they did soar, but now they're looking for a place on earth, a new place to explore. You must cast them out with the words I say and do not show your fear. Once they're gone, before you know it, more will simply appear. Continue saying the words I speak to fight the evil souls, but one false word or one fear shown, and they will swallow you whole."

"Great," Hardy thought. "No pressure."

He waited until the words he was supposed to say materialized onto the pages.

Once above but now below, it's time for you all to go, from beast to ghost and winged creatures that fly, your actions no more, will be justified. This is my home, and forever I dwell, so I cast you now back into the depths of hell.

With the utterance of those words, a large flaming portal opened up into the ground. Horrifying screams echoed around them as he repeatedly said those words. The book entity was right. As soon as each evil soul was sucked into the portal in the ground, more would appear. The wind began screaming again, so much so that the screams of the damned souls were almost drowned out. A loud yell began echoing through the forest from a distance.

"Emma Jean," Hardy yelled. "I need to get to Emma Jean!"

"If you're going to go, take me with you and repeat these words." The book entity said.

Hardy ran with all his might, still yelling the spell he had now memorized. He watched as more. "I have to keep you safe," he told the book. "I don't want to drop you, but holding you while running is hindering me. I'm going to close the book, but I will still be repeating the spell.

Hardy closed the book, folding the entity up inside and slid it into the waistline of his pants, and pulled his shirt down over top of it. He ran until he thought his chest would explode. He spotted Emma Jean's cabin and caught his second wind.

"Emma Jean!" Hardy yelled before he even got to her cabin. "Emma Jean, where are you?"

He spotted her just then coming out of her door and being blown around by the wind so hard that she could barely stand.

"The storm shelter! We have to get to the storm shelter!" she yelled as she ran in that direction.

Hardy thought then that she probably didn't understand what was really going on. This wasn't some horrific storm. This was literal hell on earth that he was fighting for. He worried about the bigfoot group but knew they had already prepared to keep themselves safe. He saw a cave when he went for what he found out to be the ceremony. He knew they were there.

A loud, evil, demonic growl came out of nowhere. Bouncing off every tree in the forest and back into Hardy's face. Emma Jean froze in her tracks and stared hard at Hardy. Neither one had ever heard anything like that coming out of the woods.

He knew that she knew then what was happening. Still yelling the spell over and over again, he ran as fast and as hard as he could. He would explain everything to her once they were safely inside the shelter. Maybe she could also say the spell, which would add a dose of extra firepower to rid them of everything.

Before Hardy could get to Emma Jean, however, he heard a soothing, female voice coming from the woods.

"Hardy, this isn't where you belong. This is all a dream. You need to wake up, Hardy."

He saw her there just beyond the trees when he stopped to see where the voice was coming from. She was beautiful. Long, dark hair, slender frame, and high-cut cheekbones. She reminded him of the daughter of the tribal leader back home. Cherokee no doubt. He was mesmerized by her looks and her energy. Everything that was going on just seemed to stop all at once at the utterance of her words. Now, he was more confused than ever. Was this really a dream? No. There's no way. Everything was just too real. He felt the book vibrating at his waistband. It brought him out of whatever trance she had him in. This evil entity knew he was no longer being pulled in. She changed then.

A scowl covered her once beautiful face. Ears grew from the top of her head through her dark hair, and fur sprouted from her slender frame. Her eyes which were once an enchanting emerald green, grew red. She laughed an evil yet maniacal laugh as all of the sounds picked back up, and she charged him as a lion would its prey.

Hardy took off running again. He just had to keep pushing past the agonizing burn in his body and the pounding of his heart. He heard Emma Jean's voice again as she yelled his name, ushering him to hurry up. He yelled the spell over and over again. Each time he repeated it, he could hear loud screeches and yells. He heard Emma Jean yelling his name. He hadn't heard it before. He was enthralled by this Lamashtu. Almost again convinced and drawn away from what he is supposed to do. He met Emma Jean at the storm shelter, and they quickly climbed inside and slammed the doors closed.

"Hardy, what is going on out there?" Emma Jean as she shook.

Hardy reached and pulled the book from the waist of his pants. He laid it on the ground and gently opened its cover, now knowing what was inside.

"The bigfoot family group did a protection ceremony for me, Emma Jean. Luna kept saying the book would tell me what to do. Even Utana said it before I left. I got home, and it revealed itself." Hardy said.

Emma Jean was bewildered at what he was saying and couldn't understand. "Hardy, are you telling me this book you found is supposed to save us?"

Hardy laughed as he flipped the pages to the middle of the book. "No, this book is literally alive."

As soon as he reached the middle pages, the book started glowing and then revealed itself to Emma Jean. She quickly sat down on some crates, fearing what just appeared in front of her.

"Don't be scared, Emma Jean, she won't hurt you. She's here to help. Luna and Utana both said the book will tell you. When I got home, that's when what they said all made sense. Maybe not the way I thought, but, nonetheless. She told me of a spell to say, and portals to the underworld would open and swallow everything up. What she said was true."

The glinting blue entity hovered above the open pages, smiling and nodding at everything Hardy was saying.

"Now, if you join me in saying it, Emma Jean, I think we can both defeat this evil and take back this portion of the mountain. Once this is done, nothing else that has any ill intent can come forward. It will again be safe for us and those who want to use its trails and camp-grounds."

He could see that she was perplexed, and he completely understood. He had just unraveled a whole nest of information that he would have difficulty deciphering.

"Can we say it in here?" Emma Jean asked.

"No, we have to be outside. I know you're scared, and trust me, I get it. I was too. But this will rid us of them forever."

Emma Jean sat quietly. She sighed as she stood up and walked over to Hardy. "Well, let's do this then." She smiled.

They slowly walked to the stairs inside the storm shelter. They could hear the wind howling, growls, and screams swirling around Emma Jean's property. They knew that Hardy was in the storm shelter. They sounded as if they were hovering right at the door. With a fearful glance towards Emma Jean, Hardy pushed the door open. The wind howled louder, and every menacing entity almost celebrated him coming out. Hardy had once again nestled the book into the waistline of his pants. Emma Jean stood behind him, muttering the words to the spell, trying to be sure not to mess up the words when they said them aloud.

They both stepped out of the shelter. Hardy reached down and grabbed her hand and smiled.

"You ready?"

"As I'll ever be, Hardy." Emma Jean said, returning the smile.

As they repeated the spell over and over again, the ground shook, and a large portal opened. The heat that emanated from it almost knocked them off their feet. They made their way to Emma Jean's deck, still repeating it. They fearfully stood watching as each evil soul was sucked into their eternity of torment. They saw movement off to the side of her cabin, and that's when they saw Utana emerging from the bushes, motioning for Hardy to come to where he stood.

"I don't think you should go over there," Emma Jean said, "What if it's a trick?"

Hardy thought about that briefly, but he was sure it was Utana. He was a pure soul who wouldn't usher him out if he thought it was unsafe for him to go, and he wouldn't be able to be overtaken because he was too spiritual. Hardy gripped Emma Jean's hand and approached Utana, hoping he would tell him something to speed up the process. This mountain had to have been full of more evil than he realized. The screams of the damned grew louder with each step.

"Utana, this is scary and more than I realized. Is there anything to do to clear out this land faster?" Hardy asked as he stood facing Utana.

Utana was quiet as he stood staring at Hardy. He wasn't saying anything, and Hardy was really taken aback by that. Utana leaned over and wrapped his arms around him. Hardy was shocked and didn't move a muscle.

"I love you too, big guy, but this really isn't the time." Hardy managed a small laugh.

Utana stood up, placed his large, burly hands around Hardy's rib cage, and lifted him off the ground.

"Hardy, no!" he heard Emma Jean yell from her deck stairs.

He made eye contact with Utana. He knew then that Emma Jean was right. It was a trap, and he fell right into it. The eyes that he stared into no longer belonged to Utana. They turned from a loving glance to something darker and more sinister, then they started to glow red. It was the Lamashtu.

"You're too trusting, you stupid man. You have fallen into every trap I have set for you," she said in an evil tone. "This almost isn't any fun for me because you're so gullible. Now, say goodbye to your beloved because you have now met your end. You lose, Hardy. I win."

With those words, she threw him into the air and raked her large claws through the center of his stomach as he fell. He felt his shirt growing wet with blood. Hardy was instantly dizzy and nauseated. He tried to hide his fear as the book entity said, but at the point he couldn't. The wind still howled as he fell. He tried to rationalize what was happening. His vision was beginning to go dark, and his stomach was almost vibrating where the claws had been. He hit the ground hard but managed to stumble to Emma Jean's feet.

Hardy, no!" Emma Jean knelt by his side, sobbing. "You bastards!" Emma Jean yelled into the woods.

The Lamashtu filled the whole area with growling echoes of maniacal laughter. "You lose, you stupid humans. You will never be able to rid this place of me or any other evil spirit."

After those words were spoken, the fiery portal closed.

Suddenly, the winds stopped blowing. There seemed to be a large hush that fell over the woods just then.

The bigfoot family, ensuring everything was safe, all walked out and over to Emma Jean and Hardy.

"Utana, please, please do something." She pleaded.

The littles ran over, and they each took his hands. Luna knelt by Hardy's head and Utana, at his feet. When Utana reached up with his long arm to lay his hand on Hardy's stomach where this evil dogman had torn into him, he stopped and stared at Luna in amazement. Emma Jean was confused. She was waiting for Utana and Luna to heal him. She couldn't hear them speaking. She didn't have that ability.

"He's not dead, Luna." Utana said.

Luna looked confused.

Utana stood up and walked to Hardy's mid-section and raised his shirt. To his surprise, it wasn't Hardy's stomach he saw. It was the book! The book that Hardy had secured into the waist of his pants as he ran. Emma Jean knelt her head on Hardy's shoulder, still sobbing, but for a different reason this time. There was only blood spilled from the deep scratches on Hardy's ribs from where this Lamashtu began to claw him. The largest and very deep gashes meant for him were instead dug deep into the book cover. Luna ran to get some large wet leaves to lay on his head. The littles snuggled up to Hardy and laid their heads on his chest. They smiled when they heard the sound of his heart beating. The weight of the little's heads and the cold water from the leaves on his face from Luna began to bring him around. They slowly got him to his feet.

He jumped back in fear when he saw Utana standing there, and rightfully so after what had just happened. His mind was a jumbled mess, and he no longer knew what was real. He didn't feel like he could trust that even Emma Jean was who he was looking at. But that was the goal of all the evil beings. To drive you to the brink of insanity. Hardy felt he was knocking at the door to that now.

"You get away from me," Hardy yelled as he backed up, wincing in pain and holding onto his side. The scratches burned, almost as if he could still feel the claws digging into him.

"Hardy, this is really Utana. You don't have to be afraid." Emma Jean said, walking towards him to try to reassure him.

Silence was all around him, with the only sounds of the screaming winds. A voice then broke through the jumbled recesses of Hardy's mind.

"You were taken advantage of," Utana spoke telepathically to him. "We did all we could to protect you. I would never harm you."

Hardy stopped where he stood and looked at Utana and the littles that clung to his legs. He shook the cobwebs from his brain and rubbed his face with his hands. His eyes began to clear, and he no longer felt like he was in a clouded vortex. He saw the mangled book lying off to the side that bore deep gashes on its cover. It was all becoming clearer to him, and he began to understand what had happened. He slowly walked back over to Emma Jean and the Bigfoot family, who were all staring at him.

Emma Jean wrapped her arms around him and kissed him. But as their two lips met, the winds howled again. The trees swayed back and forth ferociously now, more so than before. Luna ushered the littles away from Hardy and Emma Jean. The book lying on the ground flew open with loud pops and cracks from the cover being shredded. The blue entity fluttered up from the pages. The dress she had on was ripped, right at her midsection.

"The strength you've found in each other's love can heal the seam torn above. Repeat the spell with all your might, but be ready to win this fight now."

With that, the entity dissolved into the pages of the book and disappeared. The book closed with a loud thud.

Luna and Utana rushed the littles away to safety as Emma Jean and Hardy joined hands and repeated every line of the spell. The ground beneath their feet began to shake, and off to the side, a portal that was larger than the first opened up. Flames were shooting up now, ready to devour more souls, and screams and moans could be heard coming from within.

"Don't focus on that. Focus on me." Hardy told Emma Jean.

She looked into his eyes as they kept repeating the spell. Dogmen of an innumerous amount got sucked into the portal, finally revealing the host of the forest. This time, however, she was beautiful. She had long dark hair and dark eyes. A true sight to behold. But instantly, the more the spell was repeated, the ghastlier she again became. Her face looked as if it had turned inside out; fur began growing from her arms and face; nails sprung out from the tips of her fingers, and finally, she had reached her true form. An entity larger than Utana stood before them. But they never wavered.

The portal was still open, and it was time for her to go in. Hardy and Emma Jean screamed the spell at the tops of their voices. With a loud banshee call, this Lamshtu was being sucked into the portal. She fell to the ground and dug her long, black claws into the disintegrating dirt surrounding her. She tried to claw her way out. But louder and louder Hardy and Emma Jean got. With one loud final scream, she was gone. The portal closed, and once again, all was still. The clouds parted, and the sun came out. Birds began lifting their voices once again in song.

The bigfoot family emerged once again. Utana walked over to Hardy.

"Brother, friend." Utana said out loud.

Hardy laughed at the sound of Utana's deep, gravelly voice. Not the same he heard in his head. The littles ran up to Hardy and wrapped their arms around his legs. Luna smiled at Hardy as if to say thank you. Emma Jean spotted the book lying off to the side and motioned to Hardy to look at it. He walked over to the book, but as he picked it up, it turned to ash. A slight breeze blew, blowing it from his hands and into the air.

"You've done it, Hardy. Love always conquers evil. But this you had to learn in your own way. Go, live your life in harmony now." The voice of the entity said, and it was gone.

Tiffany S. Doran

AFTERWORD

Go to <u>hangaripublishing.com</u> to learn more about the Authors and stay up to date with their newest releases.

www.ingramcontent.com/pod-product-compliance
Lightning Source LLC
Chambersburg PA
CBHW071200120626
46546CB00006B/2347